Something Special Cookbook

Festive Fare for Entertaining

Margaret Happel

Butterick Publishing

Art Direction: *Remo Cosentino*
Book Design: *Binnie Weissleder*
Photography: *Gordon E. Smith*

Pictured on the front cover: Stuffed Crown Roast of Lamb (page 30).

The author and publisher thank the following for supplying props for use in the photography: Bardith, Inc., 901 Madison Avenue, New York, NY 10021; Henri Bendel, 10 West 57th Street, New York, NY 10019; Cepelia Corporation, 63 East 57th Street, New York, NY 10022; La Cuisinière, 867 Madison Avenue, New York, NY 10021; Limited Additions, Shop 66, 1050 Second Avenue, New York, NY 10022; Manhattan Ad Hoc Housewares, 842 Lexington Avenue, New York, NY 10021; Of All Things, 900 First Avenue, New York, NY 10022; Royal Copenhagen Porcelain Co., 573 Madison Avenue, New York, NY 10022; and Tibor's Antiques, Shop 76, 1050 Second Avenue, New York, NY 10022.

Library of Congress Cataloging in Publication Data

Happel, Margaret.
    Something special cookbook.

    (A PartySaver cookbook from Butterick)
    Includes index.
    1. Entertaining. 2. Cookery. 3. Menus.
I. Title. II. Series: PartySaver cookbook from Butterick.
TX731.H265   642′.41   79-24949
ISBN 0-88421-046-4

Manufactured and printed in the United States of America, published simultaneously in the USA and Canada.

CONTENTS

INTRODUCTION

Everybody loves a party! And guests enjoy themselves even more when the host or hostess is clearly having a good time, too. Whether you've invited six or sixteen-plus, the party will practically run itself if you follow the do-ahead work plans and delectable recipes in this book.

In the Something Special Cookbook *you'll find parties of every description, from classic dinner parties to a child's birthday celebration; from an old-time Thanksgiving feast to a Valentine tea; from informal brunches to elegant and sumptuous buffets.*

Whatever the event, these party-saving tips will ensure that your celebration is a smashing success.

- *Never try out a new recipe for a reputation-on-the-line party. Always make it at least once before. After you've given the dish a trial run you'll feel confident about your skill in making it.*

- *Read the work plan that prefaces each party all the way through. A good party—particularly a big one—depends on making dishes ahead, freeing you to relax and enjoy your company.*

- *Plan a shopping trip well in advance. Make sure you have everything you need to avoid last-minute panic over a missing ingredient.*

- *If you're planning to serve wine, buy or order it well ahead of time. A bottle of wine will comfortably serve three or four. White wine should be chilled; it needs at least an hour in the refrigerator. Store red wine in a cool place and open the bottle 30 minutes before serving it so the flavor and aroma, or bouquet, can develop.*

Most importantly, have fun! If you follow these suggestions you'll be all set to join the crowd and celebrate.

Dinner Parties

"Come for dinner!" *Whether your invitation is for a small, informal get-together or a full-course, sit-down dinner for eight, you'll find plenty of excellent choices among the dinner parties in this chapter.*

If you decide to polish the silver for a formal dinner party, try to keep the guest list down. Up to eight is a manageable number if you're doing all the cooking and serving yourself. Keep in mind that formality needn't mean elaborate food preparation. Excellent ingredients simply and carefully prepared will lend your party an air of sophistication. For example, tomato juice made from fresh tomatoes then simply seasoned with olive oil, wine vinegar and garlic becomes the classic cold Spanish soup, gazpacho—a perfect beginning to the Summertime Dinner featured here.

Nor does everything have to be made from scratch. Like most of today's hosts and hostesses, you probably have to sandwich your party preparations between work and family commitments. Take heart if your time is fragmented, and invest in convenience foods. A superb pâté, an excellent salad dressing, some unusual frozen or preserved fruits and vegetables, and high-quality crackers, cookies and cake mixes should all go into your supply of party staples.

The best solution to a host's time problem are the menus and work plans accompanying each dinner party in this chapter. Diverse and delicious dishes make up the menus for any occasion, from an informal Dinner for Teenagers to a festive Celebration Dinner. If you follow the work plan, everything from appetizer to dessert will be ready at just the right moment.

Send out the invitations, sure of your party-giving abilities. Formal or casual, the definitive dinner party can be found in the pages that follow.

SUMMER-TIME DINNER

GAZPACHO*

GRILLED FLANK STEAK*

BABY PEAS AND
MUSHROOMS

BAKED POTATOES

LEMON PIE

For four.

WORK PLAN: At least 4 hours before serving time, marinate Flank Steak (page 8). Prepare Gazpacho (below); chill. To make lemon pie, line one 9-inch pie plate with shortcrust pastry using a packaged mix; bake empty shell according to label directions; cool. Prepare one 3¾-ounce package instant lemon pudding and pie filling according to label directions, stirring in 1 teaspoon grated lemon rind; pour into pie shell and chill. At dessert time, top with 1 cup heavy cream, stiffly beaten and sweetened with 2 tablespoons confectioners' sugar.

About an hour before serving time, scrub 4 medium-size Idaho potatoes until very clean; prick potatoes all over with a fork and rub with vegetable oil. Bake at 400° F for 1 hour or until tender.

Thirty minutes before serving time, remove Flank Steak from refrigerator as directed. Combine two 10-ounce packages frozen peas, 2 cups sliced mushrooms, ¼ cup butter or margarine, 1 teaspoon each salt and sugar and ¼ teaspoon pepper in ovenproof casserole; cover and bake along with potatoes.

At the last moment, drain Flank Steak from marinade and broil as directed.

GAZPACHO

3 large tomatoes, peeled
1 small cucumber, sliced
½ small onion
½ green pepper, seeded
1 clove garlic, peeled
½ cup tomato juice
3 tablespoons olive oil
**2 tablespoons dried herbs
  (chives, dill, tarragon)**
1 teaspoon salt
¼ teaspoon pepper
**croutons or chopped
  cucumber (optional)**

1. Seed and quarter tomatoes; slice cucumber, onion and green pepper.

2. In electric blender, puree tomatoes, sliced cucumber, onion, green pepper, garlic, tomato juice, oil, herbs, salt and pepper.

3. Strain and chill. Stir well before serving. Garnish with croutons or chopped cucumber if desired.

GRILLED FLANK STEAK

2-pound flank steak
2 tablespoons soy sauce
2 tablespoons olive or
   vegetable oil
2 tablespoons chopped
   shallots or onion
1 tablespoon dry sherry
1 tablespoon lemon juice
1 clove garlic, crushed
¼ teaspoon crumbled thyme
⅛ teaspoon pepper

1. Trim off and discard most of fat from meat. Score meat on both sides to keep from curling.

2. In 13 x 9 x 2-inch glass dish, combine soy sauce, oil, shallots or onion, sherry, lemon juice, garlic, thyme and pepper. Stir to mix well. Place meat in dish; spoon some of marinade over meat. Cover and marinate in refrigerator for 4 to 8 hours, turning every 2 hours. Remove from refrigerator 30 minutes before broiling.

3. Preheat broiler or prepare coals for grilling.

4. Broil steak 3 inches from heat, 4 minutes per side, or grill on charcoal cooker, about 5 minutes per side. Baste with marinade when turning meat. Slice diagonally across grain; serve at once.

STEAK DINNER

STEAK

GRATED POTATO
PANCAKE *

SAVORY BRUSSELS
SPROUTS *

FRESH STRAWBERRIES
AND PINEAPPLE

SHORTBREAD *

CHOCOLATE-COVERED
MINTS

For four.

WORK PLAN: At least 2 hours before serving time, prepare Shortbread (see page 9). At the same time, wash and hull 1 pint fresh strawberries; cut in half. Peel and core a small pineapple; cut into bite-size pieces. Combine strawberries and pineapple and 1 cup sweet sherry or apricot nectar; cover and chill until ready to serve with Shortbread and mints.

Thirty minutes before serving time, prepare potatoes for Grated Potato Pancake and sprouts for Savory Brussels Sprouts; cook both 15 minutes before serving time (see recipes page 9). While pancake and sprouts cook, broil 1½-pound sirloin steak, 1 to 1½ inches thick, 4 inches from heat, 4 to 8 minutes per side. Brush each side with a mixture of ¼ cup butter or margarine, melted, and 1 teaspoon each salt, curry powder and Worcestershire sauce.

GRATED POTATO PANCAKE

1½ pounds potatoes
1 small onion
¾ teaspoon salt
¼ teaspoon pepper
¼ cup bacon fat, butter,
    margarine or vegetable oil
2 tablespoons flour

1. Peel potatoes; coarsely grate and squeeze dry in towel. There should be approximately 6 cups. Grate onion. In medium bowl, combine grated potatoes and onion with salt and pepper.

2. Melt 2 tablespoons of the fat in medium-size heavy skillet over medium heat. Using pancake turner, gently press potato mixture into 1 large patty in skillet; sauté for 10 minutes or until bottom of pancake is browned.

3. Flour a 12-inch plate; turn pancake onto plate. Add remaining 2 tablespoons fat to skillet. Slide pancake back into skillet; cook 10 minutes longer or until bottom is browned. Cut into wedges to serve.

SAVORY BRUSSELS SPROUTS

1 pint fresh Brussels sprouts
2 slices bacon
1 tablespoon chopped
    shallots or onion
¼ cup heavy cream
1 tablespoon chopped
    parsley
1 teaspoon salt
¼ teaspoon pepper

1. Wash and trim Brussels sprouts; cut an "X" in stem ends. Blanch sprouts in boiling salted water for 3 to 5 minutes; drain and set aside.

2. Fry bacon in medium skillet over medium-high heat until crisp. Drain on paper towel; crumble and set aside. Pour all but 1 tablespoon bacon fat from skillet.

3. Sauté shallots or onion in bacon fat in skillet for about 2 minutes. Add crumbled bacon, cream, parsley, salt and pepper.

4. Add Brussels sprouts; stir to coat with cream. Cook for 3 to 4 minutes or until sprouts are hot and tender.

SHORTBREAD

1 cup butter (not margarine)
¾ cup sugar
2⅓ cups flour
¼ teaspoon salt
1 teaspoon vanilla extract
1 teaspoon sugar

1. Preheat oven to 300° F.

2. In large bowl, cream butter. Gradually add ¾ cup sugar; beat until light and fluffy. Add flour and salt; mix well. Add vanilla extract.

3. Press dough into ungreased 9-inch pie plate. Cut into 12 wedges, but do not separate. Sprinkle 1 teaspoon sugar over dough.

4. Bake for 40 minutes or until firm and pale golden. Cool in pan on wire rack for 10 minutes. Carefully recut into wedges; cool completely. *Makes 12 cookies.*

INTIMATE DINNER PARTY

FRENCH BREAD WITH
SARDINE BUTTER*

GRILLED CALVES' LIVER*

BOILED NEW POTATOES

BROCCOLI AND CELERY

GREEN SALAD

APPLE CRISP*

For four.

WORK PLAN: At least 4 hours before serving time or a day ahead, make Sardine Butter (below). Serve as appetizer with warm French bread.

One hour before serving time, prepare salad by combining 2 cups each romaine lettuce pieces, endive pieces and watercress sprigs in large salad bowl; cover with plastic wrap and refrigerate. Toss with ⅓ cup vinaigrette dressing just before serving. Prepare Apple Crisp (page 11); let cool at room temperature and serve for dessert with 1 cup heavy cream, stiffly beaten.

Thirty minutes before serving time, prepare vegetables: Scrub 1 pound new potatoes and peel off a band around center of each; cook in boiling salted water until tender, about 15 minutes. Drain, and toss with 2 tablespoons each butter or margarine and chopped parsley. Cook 2 cups each fresh broccoli sprigs and 2-inch celery pieces in 1 cup chicken broth, 1½ teaspoons salt and ¼ teaspoon pepper until tender, about 15 minutes; drain before serving.

Fifteen minutes before serving time, prepare Grilled Calves' Liver (page 11).

SARDINE BUTTER

two 3¾-ounce cans
   boneless, skinless
   sardines in oil, drained
½ cup unsalted butter or
   margarine, softened
2 tablespoons cream cheese,
   softened
2 teaspoons lemon juice
½ teaspoon salt
¼ teaspoon cayenne pepper
¼ teaspoon Worcestershire
   sauce
⅛ teaspoon black pepper
1 tablespoon chopped fresh
   dill

1. Place drained sardines, butter or margarine, cream cheese, lemon juice, salt, cayenne, Worcestershire sauce and black pepper in medium bowl. Using electric mixer at low speed, mix for 1 minute or until well blended.

2. Turn mixture into 4 individual butter crocks if used as first course, or into larger dish if used as hors d'oeuvre. Top with dill.

Note: This is best if made a day ahead. Cover with plastic wrap and refrigerate until ready to serve.

GRILLED CALVES' LIVER

6 slices bacon
3 tablespoons butter or
  margarine
2 cups thinly sliced onions
6 slices calves' liver (about
  1½ pounds)
flour
1 teaspoon salt
¼ teaspoon pepper

1. Fry bacon in 12-inch grilling skillet (iron skillet with ridges) or large heavy skillet over medium heat until crisp. Drain on paper towels; crumble and set aside.

2. Add 1 tablespoon of the butter or margarine to hot fat in skillet; add onions and sauté for 5 minutes, until soft. Remove with slotted spoon to heated serving platter; keep warm.

3. Wipe liver with damp paper towels. Lightly flour liver slices; season with salt and pepper.

4. Add 1 tablespoon of the butter or margarine to skillet; heat over medium-high heat until very hot. Add liver, 2 or 3 slices at a time, and sauté 1 minute per side or until brown outside but still slightly pink inside. Remove as browned to heated serving platter and keep warm. Add remaining butter or margarine to skillet as needed.

5. To serve liver, top with onions and sprinkle with crumbled bacon.

APPLE CRISP

4 cups sliced, peeled tart
  apples
2 tablespoons granulated
  sugar
1 tablespoon lemon juice
1 teaspoon grated lemon
  rind

TOPPING
½ cup butter or margarine,
  softened
1 cup flour
1 cup dark brown sugar,
  firmly packed
1 teaspoon cinnamon
¼ teaspoon nutmeg

1. Preheat oven to 325° F.

2. Place 2 cups of the apples in greased 9-inch pie plate. Sprinkle with granulated sugar, lemon juice and lemon rind. Add remaining 2 cups apples.

3. To make topping, cream butter or margarine in large bowl. Add flour, brown sugar, cinnamon and nutmeg. Stir to blend well.

4. Spread butter mixture evenly over apples. Press down around edge of pie plate. Cut several slits in top to allow steam to escape. Bake for 35 to 45 minutes or until topping is well browned.

Note: This recipe serves four very generously.

TWO-COUPLE DINNER

BROILED CHICKEN*

RICE WITH MUSHROOMS

CAULIFLOWER AND PEAS*

ICE CREAM WITH PEAR SLICES*

For four.

WORK PLAN: At least 3 hours before serving time, place chicken in marinade (see Broiled Chicken recipe below).

Forty-five minutes before serving time, prepare Pear Slices (page 13); make sauce at dessert time and serve as directed with ice cream.

About 30 minutes before serving time, cook Broiled Chicken as directed. At the same time, prepare Cauliflower and Peas (page 13) and keep warm. For rice with mushrooms, melt 2 tablespoons butter or margarine in medium skillet; add 1 cup sliced mushrooms and sauté until just tender, about 3 minutes. Add 1 cup long-grain rice and cook according to label directions, using chicken broth as the liquid instead of water.

BROILED CHICKEN

two 3-pound broiler-fryer
  chickens, quartered
¾ cup soy sauce
¾ cup dry sherry
2 cloves garlic, quartered
1 tablespoon lemon juice
¼ teaspoon crumbled thyme
⅛ teaspoon pepper
3 tablespoons butter or
  margarine, melted

1. Remove tail pieces, back bones and wing tips from chicken quarters. Wash chicken quarters under cold running water; pat dry with paper towels.

2. In a 13 x 9 x 2-inch glass dish, combine soy sauce, sherry, garlic, lemon juice, thyme and pepper. Add chicken; marinate for 3 to 6 hours, turning once or twice.

3. Preheat broiler to 400° F.

4. Place chicken quarters skin side down on rack in broiling pan. Brush with melted butter or margarine. Broil 4 inches from heat for 10 to 15 minutes, basting twice with pan drippings. Reduce heat if necessary to avoid burning.

5. Turn chicken; baste. Broil 10 minutes longer, until juices run clear when meat is pierced with two-tined fork. Pour pan drippings over chicken to serve.

CAULIFLOWER AND PEAS

2 cups chicken broth
1 head cauliflower, broken into flowerets
1 pound fresh peas, shelled
1 small onion, sliced
1 cup unflavored yogurt
1 teaspoon lemon juice
1 teaspoon chopped fresh dill
½ teaspoon salt
⅛ teaspoon pepper

1. Bring chicken broth to boiling point in large saucepan; add cauliflower and simmer, covered, for 15 minutes, until tender. Remove cauliflower with slotted spoon and set aside.

2. Add peas and onion to broth in pan; simmer, covered, for 5 minutes, until tender. Remove with slotted spoon and set aside.

3. Raise heat to high and reduce broth to 1 cup. Reduce heat to low; stir in yogurt, lemon juice, dill, salt and pepper. Return vegetables to saucepan; heat thoroughly but do not boil.

ICE CREAM WITH PEAR SLICES

4 ripe pears, peeled, cored and cut lengthwise into eighths
¼ cup lemon juice
¼ cup butter or margarine
3 tablespoons brown sugar
1 tablespoon pear liqueur or kirsch
1½ pints vanilla ice cream
¼ teaspoon nutmeg

1. In large bowl, soak sliced pears for 30 minutes in cold water to cover along with 2 tablespoons of the lemon juice. Drain pears and pat dry with paper towels.

2. Melt butter or margarine in medium-size enameled or stainless steel skillet over medium heat; add remaining 2 tablespoons lemon juice and the brown sugar and heat until brown sugar dissolves.

3. Add pears; cook for 5 minutes, stirring gently with wooden spoon. Remove pears to heated plate; keep warm.

4. Just before serving, add liqueur to skillet. Raise heat to high and cook sauce, stirring constantly, until it thickens.

5. Arrange pear slices on individual plates. Place 1 or 2 scoops vanilla ice cream on each serving, pour sauce over ice cream and sprinkle nutmeg on top.

UPTOWN DINNER

ROCK CORNISH HENS
WITH CHERRY SAUCE *

DINNER ROLLS *

CREAMED SPINACH

SPICE CAKE

For four.

WORK PLAN: Three hours before serving time, prepare Dinner Rolls (page 15). Make spice cake by preparing one 18.5-ounce yellow cake mix according to label directions, adding 1 teaspoon each cinnamon and ginger. Bake and cool cake as directed; fill and frost with 2 cups buttercream frosting spiced with 1 teaspoon each cinnamon and ginger and ¼ teaspoon each nutmeg and allspice (use a 16-ounce can frosting if desired). Chill until serving time.

One hour before serving time, prepare Rock Cornish Hens with Cherry Sauce (below). While game hens bake, wash and trim 2 pounds fresh spinach; place in large saucepan with water clinging to leaves, adding 2 tablespoons butter or margarine, 1½ teaspoons salt and ½ teaspoon each pepper and nutmeg. Cook over very low heat until spinach is tender; stir in ½ cup heavy cream and heat, but do not boil.

ROCK CORNISH HENS WITH CHERRY SAUCE

4 Rock Cornish hens
4 Rock Cornish hen livers
1 tablespoon vegetable oil
½ cup chopped onion
¼ cup dry vermouth
**3 cups packaged herb
   stuffing mix**
½ cup chicken broth
**1 tablespoon chopped
   parsley**
**½ teaspoon grated lemon
   rind**
½ teaspoon tarragon
¼ teaspoon salt
⅛ teaspoon pepper
¼ cup butter or margarine
Cherry Sauce (page 15)

1. Wash Cornish hens under cold running water; pat dry with paper towels and set aside.

2. Chop livers. Heat oil in small skillet over medium heat; add livers and onion and sauté for 5 minutes. Add vermouth; simmer for 3 minutes.

3. In large bowl, combine liver mixture with stuffing mix, broth, parsley, lemon rind, tarragon, salt and pepper. Stuff Cornish hens with liver mixture. Melt butter or margarine.

4. Place hens on wire rack in roasting pan. Bake at 350° F for 35 to 45 minutes, basting every 10 minutes with melted butter or margarine and pan drippings, until juices run clear when thigh is pierced with two-tined fork.

5. Meanwhile, make Cherry Sauce. Serve with hens.

Cherry Sauce

3 tablespoons sugar
1 tablespoon cornstarch
¼ teaspoon salt
¼ teaspoon dry mustard
½ cup chicken broth
½ cup orange juice
one 20-ounce can pitted
    sour cherries
1 orange, peeled, seeded
    and coarsely chopped

1. In small saucepan, mix sugar, cornstarch, salt and dry mustard. Add chicken broth, orange juice and liquid from cherries.

2. Cook over medium heat, stirring constantly, until sauce thickens and bubbles, about 3 minutes. Just before serving, add cherries and orange. *Makes about 3 cups.*

DINNER ROLLS

2 packages active dry yeast
1 tablespoon sugar
¼ cup very warm water
1 cup milk, scalded and
    cooled
½ cup sugar
¼ cup butter or margarine
¼ cup vegetable shortening
1 teaspoon salt
1 egg
4 cups flour

1. Dissolve yeast and 1 tablespoon sugar in very warm water (which feels comfortably warm when dropped on wrist); let stand until bubbly, about 10 minutes. Let cool to lukewarm.

2. In large bowl, combine cooled yeast mixture, cooled milk, ½ cup sugar, the butter or margarine, shortening and salt; stir to mix well. Beat in egg.

3. Beat in enough flour to make a soft dough. Turn out onto lightly floured pastry cloth or board. Knead dough for 7 to 10 minutes, until smooth and elastic.

4. Place dough in greased large bowl; turn to grease all sides. Cover with plastic wrap and a clean towel. Let rise in warm, draft-free place for 1½ hours or until doubled in bulk.

5. Form dough into rolls of desired shape (round, rectangular or folded over) about 1½ inches wide. Place in greased 13 x 9 x 2-inch baking pan. Cover pan with clean towel. Let rolls rise in warm, draft-free place for 1 hour or until doubled in bulk.

6. Ten minutes before end of rising time, preheat oven to 425° F. Bake rolls for 10 to 12 minutes or until golden. Serve warm. *Makes 18.*

CELEBRATION DINNER

CRABMEAT WITH
MUSHROOMS*

ASPARAGUS

TOMATOES WITH CURRY
DRESSING*

DATE-FILLED BAKED
APPLES*

For four.

WORK PLAN: At least 4 hours before serving time or a day ahead, prepare Curry Dressing for tomatoes (see recipe page 17).

One hour before serving time, prepare Date-Filled Baked Apples (page 17); keep warm until dessert time.

Thirty minutes before serving, assemble Tomatoes with Curry Dressing as directed. Make Crabmeat with Mushrooms (below). Then wash and peel 1 pound fresh asparagus; add asparagus and 1 teaspoon sugar to ½ inch boiling salted water in large skillet and cook until tender, about 5 to 7 minutes. (Or prepare two 10-ounce packages frozen asparagus spears according to label directions.)

CRABMEAT WITH MUSHROOMS

3 tablespoons butter or
  margarine
3 cups sliced mushrooms
1 cup sliced green onions
3 tablespoons flour
2 tablespoons chopped
  parsley
1 tablespoon lemon juice
¼ cup dry vermouth
one 16-ounce container sour
  cream
3 cups fresh crabmeat,
  picked over, or 3 cups
  frozen crabmeat, thawed,
  drained and cartilage
  removed
1 teaspoon salt
¼ teaspoon pepper
¼ teaspoon nutmeg
2 drops hot pepper sauce
4 English muffins, split and
  toasted

1. Melt butter or margarine in large skillet over medium heat; add mushrooms and green onions and sauté for 3 minutes.

2. Add flour, parsley and lemon juice; stir to mix well. Add vermouth; cook, stirring constantly, until mixture thickens and bubbles, about 3 minutes. Reduce heat to low. Stir in sour cream; do not allow to boil.

3. Add crabmeat, salt, pepper, nutmeg and hot pepper sauce. Heat thoroughly but do not boil. Serve on toasted English muffins.

TOMATOES WITH CURRY DRESSING

**2 tablespoons chopped
  onion**
½ cup mayonnaise
½ cup sour cream
½ teaspoon curry powder
¼ teaspoon salt
⅛ teaspoon pepper
**4 ripe tomatoes, sliced
lettuce leaves**

1. Press onion in garlic press to make 2 teaspoons onion juice.

2. In medium bowl, combine onion juice, mayonnaise, sour cream, curry, salt and pepper. Pour dressing into screwtop jar; cover. Refrigerate for up to 24 hours before serving.

3. Arrange tomatoes on individual salad plates lined with lettuce leaves. Shake dressing and pour over tomatoes.

DATE-FILLED BAKED APPLES

4 large tart cooking apples
1 cup chopped dates
**1 cup water, or ½ cup each
  sherry and water**

SAUCE
**one 10-ounce jar red currant
  preserves**
¼ cup sherry or orange juice

1. Core apples and prick skins well with fork; place in well-greased 12 x 8 x 2-inch baking dish.

2. Fill centers of apples with dates. Pour water or combination of sherry and water into dish; bake at 350° F for 45 minutes or until apples are tender.

3. To make sauce, heat preserves with ¼ cup sherry or orange juice in small saucepan. Serve warm over warm apples.

Sherry is an excellent commodity to have on hand for rendering both desserts and entrées particularly palatable. For the Date-Filled Baked Apples, above, you can use a medium-dry, an amontillado or a sweet sherry, depending upon how sweet a sauce you're after. A bottle of pale dry or cocktail sherry is just the thing to have on hand for main-dish sauces. Domestic sherries are less expensive than imported and are excellent for both cooking and drinking; try experimenting with different brands and degrees of dryness.

INFORMAL DINNER

MARINATED RAW SCALLOPS*

CHEESE FONDUE*

FRESH ORANGE COMPOTE

DOUBLE-FROSTED CHOCOLATE BARS*

For four.

WORK PLAN: About 3 hours before serving time, prepare Double-Frosted Chocolate Bars (page 19). At the same time, make orange compote by peeling 6 large oranges and slicing them crosswise; place slices in large shallow dessert bowl. Add 1 cup sweet sherry or fresh orange juice; cover and chill until serving time.

About 2 hours before serving time, prepare Marinated Raw Scallops (below).

Fifteen minutes before serving time, prepare Cheese Fondue (page 19). *Pictured on page 50.*

MARINATED RAW SCALLOPS

1 pound sea scallops
juice of 6 limes
1 cup thinly sliced mushrooms
½ cup thinly sliced celery
½ cup thinly sliced green pepper
¼ cup thinly sliced green onion
2 tablespoons chopped parsley
¼ cup olive oil
½ teaspoon salt
¼ teaspoon Worcestershire sauce
⅛ teaspoon pepper
3 to 4 drops hot pepper sauce

1. Rinse scallops in cold water; pat dry with paper towels. Slice into quarters. Place in small bowl; cover with lime juice. Cover bowl and marinate for at least 1 hour in refrigerator. Drain from marinade, reserving 2 tablespoons of the lime juice.

2. In large bowl, combine mushrooms, celery, green pepper, green onion and parsley. Add oil, salt, Worcestershire sauce, pepper and hot pepper sauce; mix well. Stir in reserved lime juice. Gently stir in scallops; refrigerate for 30 minutes.

3. To serve, arrange scallop mixture attractively on small chilled plates.

CHEESE FONDUE

12 ounces Emmenthaler cheese, grated
12 ounces Gruyère cheese, grated
1 clove garlic, peeled
1¼ cups dry vermouth
2 teaspoons cornstarch
⅓ cup kirsch
¼ teaspoon salt
¼ teaspoon nutmeg
⅛ teaspoon hot paprika
⅛ teaspoon pepper
2 loaves French bread

1. Blend Emmenthaler and Gruyère cheeses. Rub inside of 3- to 4-quart fondue pot or heavy saucepan with garlic.

2. Heat vermouth in same pot on stove over medium-high heat to just below boiling point. Add cheese by the cupful, stirring constantly with wooden spoon. Stir until cheese is completely melted.

3. In small bowl, blend cornstarch with kirsch; add to cheese mixture. Cook for 2 minutes, stirring constantly. Add salt, nutmeg, paprika and pepper.

4. Cut bread into bite-size cubes. All pieces should have crust.

5. Place pot on alcohol burner on table. Use long forks to pierce bread and dip into fondue.

Note: Instead of Emmenthaler and Gruyère cheese, use 1½ pounds Swiss cheese if desired. Thin slices of country ham or prosciutto are a good accompaniment to fondue.

DOUBLE-FROSTED CHOCOLATE BARS

CHOCOLATE LAYER
one 1-ounce square unsweetened chocolate
¼ cup butter or margarine
1 egg
½ cup granulated sugar
⅛ teaspoon almond extract
¼ cup flour
¼ cup chopped pecans

FROSTING
2 tablespoons butter or margarine, softened
1 cup confectioners' sugar
1 tablespoon heavy cream
¼ teaspoon vanilla extract

GLAZE
one 1-ounce square unsweetened chocolate
1 tablespoon butter or margarine

1. Preheat oven to 350° F.

2. To make chocolate layer, melt 1 square chocolate and ¼ cup butter or margarine in top of double boiler over hot water. Remove from heat and let cool slightly.

3. Using wire whisk, beat egg in medium bowl until foamy. Stir in cooled chocolate mixture, granulated sugar and almond extract. Add flour and pecans; stir to blend well. Pour into greased 8 x 8 x 2-inch baking pan.

4. Bake for 15 minutes or until wooden toothpick inserted in center comes out clean. Cool in pan on wire rack.

5. To make frosting, combine 2 tablespoons softened butter or margarine, the confectioners' sugar, cream and vanilla extract in medium bowl. Spread over cooled chocolate layer in pan. Chill for at least 10 minutes.

6. To make glaze, melt 1 square chocolate and 1 tablespoon butter or margarine in top of double boiler over hot water. Pour over chilled filling; tilt pan to coat evenly. Chill for 15 minutes; cut into 2 x 1-inch bars. *Makes 24.*

DINNER WITH OLD FRIENDS

STUFFED MUSHROOMS*

BONELESS RIB ROAST

SKILLET PEPPERS AND TOMATOES*

ROAST POTATOES

ORANGE CAKE* AND FRESH STRAWBERRIES

For six.

WORK PLAN: Several hours ahead of time, prepare Orange Cake (page 21). Serve in thin slices accompanied by 2 pints washed, hulled, sliced strawberries that have been sweetened with ¼ cup confectioners' sugar and chilled before serving.

One and a half hours before serving time, place a 4-pound boneless rib roast on wire rack in roasting pan; rub all surfaces with 1½ teaspoons salt and ½ teaspoon pepper, and brush all over with 2 tablespoons Dijon-style mustard. Roast at 350° F for 1 hour and 20 minutes to 1 hour and 45 minutes. Let stand for 10 minutes before carving. Meanwhile, peel 1½ pounds potatoes and parboil for 15 minutes; place around beef during last 30 minutes of cooking time, turning occasionally. Prepare Stuffed Mushrooms (below) and bake with beef. Make Skillet Peppers and Tomatoes (page 21).

STUFFED MUSHROOMS

12 large mushrooms
3 tablespoons butter or margarine
½ cup thinly sliced green onions
one 6½-ounce package frozen crabmeat, thawed, drained and cartilage removed
1 tablespoon dry sherry
1 tablespoon flour
½ cup heavy cream
1 egg yolk
½ teaspoon salt
⅛ teaspoon pepper
4 drops hot pepper sauce
¼ cup grated Swiss cheese

1. Preheat oven to 350° F.

2. Wipe mushrooms clean with damp paper towels; remove stems and chop finely. Set mushroom caps aside.

3. Melt 2 tablespoons of the butter or margarine in medium skillet over medium heat; add mushroom stems and green onions and sauté for 3 to 5 minutes. Add crabmeat and sherry; stir to mix well. Reduce heat to low; add flour and cook for 2 to 3 minutes, stirring constantly. Slowly stir in cream and cook until thick and bubbly. Add egg yolk, salt, pepper and hot pepper sauce.

4. Meanwhile, melt remaining 1 tablespoon butter or margarine in 13 x 9 x 2-inch baking dish by placing in preheating oven for 2 minutes. Place mushroom caps in dish, turning to coat with melted butter or margarine. Bake for 5 minutes. Let cool slightly. Heap crab mixture into mushrooms; sprinkle with grated cheese. Bake for 10 to 15 minutes, until very hot.

SKILLET PEPPERS AND TOMATOES

3 tablespoons vegetable oil
6 cups coarsely chopped
    green peppers
2 cups coarsely chopped
    onions
two 28-ounce cans Italian-
    style tomatoes, drained
1 tablespoon tomato paste
1 tablespoon salt
1 teaspoon sugar
1 teaspoon basil
¼ teaspoon pepper

1. Heat oil in large saucepan over medium heat; add green peppers and onions and sauté until soft and tender, about 10 minutes.

2. Add drained tomatoes, tomato paste, salt, sugar, basil and pepper. Stir to mix well. Reduce heat to low; simmer, covered, for 10 minutes, stirring occasionally.

ORANGE CAKE

1 cup butter or margarine,
    softened
1 cup sugar
3 eggs, separated
2 cups flour
1 teaspoon baking powder
1 teaspoon baking soda
¼ teaspoon salt
1 cup sour cream
1½ teaspoons grated orange
    rind
½ cup chopped pecans

SYRUP
½ cup sugar
½ cup orange liqueur
¼ cup orange juice

confectioners' sugar

1. Preheat oven to 350° F.

2. Using electric mixer at medium speed, beat butter or margarine, 1 cup sugar and the egg yolks in large bowl until light and fluffy.

3. Sift together flour, baking powder, baking soda and salt. With mixer at low speed, add dry ingredients alternately with sour cream to butter-sugar mixture. Stir until smooth; add orange rind and pecans. Clean beaters well.

4. Using electric mixer at high speed, beat egg whites in large bowl until stiff; fold into cake batter. Pour into greased 10-inch tube or bundt pan.

5. Bake for 45 to 50 minutes or until cake tester inserted in center comes out clean. Cool cake in pan on wire rack for 5 minutes; invert onto rack set over jelly-roll pan.

6. Meanwhile, make syrup by combining ½ cup sugar, the orange liqueur and orange juice in small saucepan. Heat just to dissolve sugar. Prick warm cake all over with cake tester; spoon warm syrup over cake. Serve cake when cool; sprinkle with some confectioners' sugar just before serving. *Makes one 10-inch tube cake.*

WINTER DINNER PARTY

BEEF BRISKET*

BUTTERED CARROTS

MUSHROOM SALAD

CHERRY TORTE*

For six.

WORK PLAN: About 6 hours before serving time, prepare Cherry Torte (page 23).

About 3½ hours before serving time, prepare Beef Brisket (below).

One hour before serving time, make salad: Wipe 2 pounds mushrooms very clean; slice thinly and divide among 6 salad platters. Sprinkle each portion with ¼ cup chopped parsley, spoon 2 to 3 tablespoons spiced herbed dressing over each and chill.

Thirty minutes before serving time, peel 2 pounds carrots and cut them into 2-inch julienne strips. Cook in boiling salted water until tender; drain, and toss with ½ cup butter or margarine.

BEEF BRISKET

5-pound fresh beef brisket
1 tablespoon vegetable oil
2 teaspoons coarse salt
½ teaspoon paprika
2 cups coarsely chopped
   onions
2 cloves garlic, crushed
2 teaspoons green
   peppercorns, crushed
½ cup dry vermouth
4 stalks celery, cut into
   2-inch pieces
6 large potatoes, peeled and
   quartered

1. Trim off and discard fat from meat. Heat oil in large ovenproof skillet or casserole over medium heat; add meat and brown, 4 minutes per side. Remove meat to large plate; sprinkle with salt and paprika.

2. Add onions and garlic to drippings in skillet or casserole; sauté for 2 minutes. Add crushed peppercorns and vermouth. Bring to boiling point; return meat to pan.

3. Cover and place in 325° F oven; bake for about 1½ hours, turning meat once. Meat will shrink slightly. Add celery and potatoes. Cook 1 to 1½ hours longer, until meat and vegetables are tender. Slice meat and serve with vegetables.

CHERRY TORTE

CRUST
1¼ cups flour
¼ cup granulated sugar
¼ teaspoon salt
½ cup butter or margarine
2 egg yolks, beaten
1 teaspoon vanilla extract

FILLING
one 8-ounce package cream
   cheese, softened
½ cup confectioners' sugar
2 tablespoons milk
1 teaspoon lemon juice

TOPPING
¾ cup granulated sugar
2 tablespoons cornstarch
⅛ teaspoon cloves
¼ teaspoon almond extract
one 20-ounce can pitted
   sour cherries

1. Preheat oven to 350° F.

2. To make crust, combine flour, ¼ cup granulated sugar and the salt in large bowl. Add butter or margarine, beaten egg yolks and vanilla extract. Using electric mixer at medium speed, blend ingredients; press into greased 9-inch pie plate, pushing up to cover sides. Bake for 20 to 25 minutes, until lightly browned; cool on wire rack.

3. To make filling, use electric mixer at high speed to combine cream cheese, confectioners' sugar, milk and lemon juice in medium bowl until light and fluffy. Spread over cooled crust; chill for 1 hour.

4. To make topping, combine ¾ cup granulated sugar, the cornstarch, cloves and almond extract in small saucepan. Drain juice from cherries and add juice to topping mixture, reserving cherries. Cook mixture over low heat until thick and glossy. Stir in cherries.

5. Cool cherry mixture. Pour over cream cheese filling. Refrigerate until ready to serve. *Makes one 9-inch pie.*

A simple dinner party like this one, carefully prepared for good, compatible friends, can do wonders for brightening up midwinter spirits. To make the occasion extra-special, serve a couple of bottles of a good, hearty red wine—domestic or imported—like a Burgundy, St. Emilion or Pinot Noir. And to further warm the cockles of their hearts, brew a big pot of freshly ground coffee to accompany dessert and after-dinner talk—a lovely ending to a convivial evening.

DINNER FOR TEENAGERS

BEEF AND RICE
MEATBALLS*

GREEN BEANS

FRENCH BREAD

SPICY FRUIT SALAD*

BROWNIES WITH ICE
CREAM AND FUDGE
SAUCE*

For six.

WORK PLAN: About 2 hours before serving time, prepare Brownies (see recipe page 25). At the same time, make Spicy Fruit Salad (page 25); chill dressing and salad separately and combine just before serving, as directed. Prepare Beef and Rice Meatballs (below).

Fifteen minutes before serving time, wash and trim 2 pounds fresh green beans; cook in boiling salted water to cover until tender, about 8 minutes. (Or prepare one 32-ounce polybag frozen whole green beans according to label directions.) Drain beans and toss with ¼ cup butter or margarine. At the same time, wrap one 18-inch-long French bread loaf in aluminum foil and heat alongside meatballs.

Finish dessert at the last moment by topping Brownies with Ice Cream and Fudge Sauce.

BEEF AND RICE MEATBALLS

one 46-ounce can tomato
  juice
½ cup chopped celery leaves
¼ cup chopped onion
1 tablespoon celery seed
1 tablespoon curry powder
1 tablespoon Worcestershire
  sauce
2 teaspoons lemon juice
1 bay leaf
2 teaspoons salt
1½ pounds ground beef
¾ cup uncooked long-grain
  rice
¾ cup chopped onion
¾ cup chopped celery
2 eggs, slightly beaten
3 tablespoons chopped
  parsley
1 tablespoon prepared mild
  mustard
2 teaspoons salt

1. Combine tomato juice, celery leaves, ¼ cup chopped onion, the celery seed, curry, Worcestershire sauce, lemon juice and bay leaf in medium saucepan. Bring to boiling point over high heat; reduce heat to medium. Cover partially; simmer for 15 minutes. Strain; add 2 teaspoons salt.

2. Meanwhile, combine ground beef, rice, ¾ cup chopped onion, the celery, slightly beaten eggs, parsley, mustard and 2 teaspoons salt in large bowl; form into balls about 1½ inches in diameter.

3. Cover bottom of 13 x 9 x 2-inch baking dish with 2 cups of the sauce. Add meatballs; cover with remaining sauce. Cover pan with aluminum foil. Bake at 350° F for about 1 hour or until rice is tender.

SPICY FRUIT SALAD

⅓ cup honey
⅓ cup vinegar
¼ cup sugar
1 tablespoon lemon juice
1 teaspoon dry mustard
1 teaspoon paprika
1 teaspoon celery seed
1 teaspoon salt
1 cup vegetable oil
6 lettuce leaves
3 cups fresh or canned
  grapefruit sections
3 cups orange sections

1. In medium bowl, combine honey, vinegar, sugar, lemon juice, dry mustard, paprika, celery seed and salt. Mix well with fork or wire whisk. Gradually add oil, stirring constantly. Chill until serving time.

2. Place 1 lettuce leaf on each of 6 salad plates. Top with grapefruit and orange sections; chill until serving time.

3. Just before serving, stir dressing; pour ⅓ cup over each portion.

BROWNIES WITH ICE CREAM AND FUDGE SAUCE

five 1-ounce squares
  unsweetened chocolate
½ cup butter or margarine
4 eggs
¼ teaspoon salt
2¼ cups sugar
1 teaspoon vanilla extract
¼ teaspoon almond extract
1 cup flour
Fudge Sauce (below)
1 quart vanilla ice cream

1. Preheat oven to 325° F. Grease and flour 13 x 9 x 2-inch baking pan.

2. Melt chocolate and butter or margarine in top of double boiler over hot water.

3. Using electric mixer at high speed, beat eggs and salt in large bowl until light and fluffy. Gradually add sugar; continue beating until mixture is pale and creamy.

4. Beat in melted chocolate mixture and vanilla and almond extracts until well blended. Stir in flour; blend well. Pour batter into prepared pan.

5. Bake for 20 to 25 minutes, until cake tester inserted in center comes out clean. Cool in pan on wire rack for 10 minutes. Cut into 24 bars.

6. Make Fudge Sauce; top six of the brownies with ice cream and sauce; store remaining brownies in airtight container.

Fudge Sauce

three 1-ounce squares
  unsweetened chocolate
1 egg, beaten
1 cup heavy cream
1 cup sugar
1 teaspoon vanilla extract

1. Melt chocolate over warm water in top of double boiler.

2. In small bowl, combine egg, cream and sugar; add to melted chocolate and stir to mix well. Cook over warm water for 15 minutes, stirring once or twice. Remove from heat. Beat sauce with wooden spoon for 1 minute. Stir in vanilla extract. *Makes about 2 cups.*

EASY DINNER PARTY

CELERY ROOT IN
MUSTARD SAUCE*

OVEN-BAKED BEEF
STEW*

BUTTERED NOODLES

GREEN SALAD

LIME SHERBET* WITH
HOMEMADE SUGAR
COOKIES*

For six.

WORK PLAN: At least 5 hours before serving time or the day before, prepare Homemade Sugar Cookies (page 28) and Celery Root in Mustard Sauce (below).

Four hours before serving, prepare Oven-Baked Beef Stew (page 27) and Lime Sherbet (page 28).

One hour before serving time, combine 3 cups each bite-size pieces salad greens and sliced peeled cucumbers in large salad bowl; cover and chill. Toss with ½ cup garlic dressing just before serving.

Ten minutes before serving time, cook one 16-ounce package wide egg noodles according to label directions; drain, and toss with 2 tablespoons butter or margarine. Serve beef stew over buttered noodles.

CELERY ROOT IN MUSTARD SAUCE

2 celery roots (about 2
  pounds)
1 tablespoon salt
1 tablespoon lemon juice
½ cup Dijon-style mustard
¼ cup boiling water
⅔ cup vegetable oil
¼ cup tarragon vinegar
1 teaspoon Worcestershire
  sauce
¼ teaspoon pepper
¼ teaspoon crumbled
  tarragon
watercress sprigs
additional crumbled
  tarragon (optional)

1. Peel celery root. With food processor or by hand, cut into 2 x ⅛-inch strips.

2. In large bowl, combine salt and lemon juice. Stir in celery root. Let stand for 30 minutes, stirring twice. Remove celery root and discard salted lemon juice; set bowl aside. Rinse celery root with cold water; drain in colander and pat dry with paper towels.

3. Add mustard to same large bowl. Gradually add boiling water, stirring constantly. Add oil and vinegar, stirring constantly. When sauce is thick and well mixed, add Worcestershire sauce, pepper and ¼ teaspoon tarragon. Stir well. Stir celery root into sauce; cover and chill for at least 4 hours or overnight.

4. To serve, spoon celery root onto individual salad plates; garnish each with a sprig or two of watercress. Sprinkle additional tarragon on top if desired.

OVEN-BAKED BEEF STEW

4½-pound beef shank
½ cup bacon fat or vegetable
  oil
2 cups sliced onions
3 cloves garlic, crushed
3 tablespoons brown sugar
1 tablespoon salt
½ teaspoon pepper
1½ cups beef broth
3 cups beer
6 sprigs parsley
2 bay leaves
½ teaspoon crumbled thyme
¼ teaspoon crumbled
  marjoram
3 tablespoons vinegar
2 tablespoons cornstarch
1 teaspoon dry mustard

1. Cut meat from shank bones into 2 x ½-inch chunks. Reserve bones.

2. Heat 2 tablespoons of the bacon fat or oil in large skillet over high heat; add one-third of meat and bones and brown. Remove from skillet to 5-quart heatproof casserole. Repeat process twice to brown remaining meat and bones.

3. Reduce heat to medium. Add remaining 2 tablespoons fat or oil to skillet; add onions and sauté for 5 minutes. Add garlic; cook 5 minutes longer.

4. Add onion mixture to meat and bones in casserole. Stir in brown sugar, salt, pepper and beef broth. Add beer.

5. Wrap parsley, bay leaves, thyme and marjoram in cheesecloth; tie with string and place in casserole. Cover casserole and bring stew to boiling point over medium heat.

6. Place casserole in 325° F oven; cook for about 2 hours or until meat is fork-tender. If necessary, reduce oven temperature so stew barely simmers.

7. Remove from oven; discard bones and herb packet. Remove meat and onions with slotted spoon; reserve. Refrigerate sauce for 30 minutes; remove fat that floats to top. (Or skim fat from surface of hot sauce with shallow spoon.) Reheat sauce in same casserole over medium heat.

8. In small bowl, combine vinegar and cornstarch. Stir into sauce. Add dry mustard; stir to mix well. Return meat and onions to sauce. Cook until mixture thickens and bubbles and meat and onions are heated through, about 3 minutes.

Note: Oven-Baked Beef Stew can be served over hot buttered egg noodles or spinach noodles. It is also delectable with fluffy long-grain rice or nutty brown rice.

LIME SHERBET

¾ cup lime juice
⅔ cup sugar
1 teaspoon grated lime rind
1 cup milk
1 cup heavy cream
2 drops green food coloring
   (optional)

1. In 1-quart metal bowl, combine lime juice, sugar and lime rind. Slowly add milk and cream, stirring until sugar dissolves. Add food coloring if desired.

2. Place in freezer until partially frozen, about 1 hour. Remove from freezer and beat until mixture is smooth. Cover with aluminum foil; return to freezer for at least 3 hours, until sherbet is solid.

Note: Lime Sherbet is delicious topped with puree of fresh pineapple or melon.

HOMEMADE SUGAR COOKIES

5 cups flour
1 teaspoon baking soda
1 teaspoon cream of tartar
½ teaspoon salt
1 cup confectioners' sugar
1 cup granulated sugar
1 cup vegetable oil
1 cup butter or margarine
2 eggs
1 tablespoon vanilla extract
additional granulated sugar

1. Sift flour, baking soda, cream of tartar and salt onto waxed paper.

2. Using electric mixer at high speed, cream confectioners' sugar, 1 cup granulated sugar, the oil and butter or margarine in large bowl until light and fluffy. Add eggs one at a time, beating well after each addition. Beat in vanilla extract until well blended.

3. Gradually stir in flour mixture. Wrap dough in waxed paper and chill for 1 hour.

4. Preheat oven to 350° F.

5. Form dough into balls about 1 inch in diameter. Place on ungreased cookie sheet. Dip bottom of small glass or butter press into extra granulated sugar; press down on cookies to flatten and make design. Continue dipping glass or press into sugar as cookies are pressed. Sprinkle cookies with more sugar.

6. Bake for 10 minutes, until lightly browned. Cool for 1 minute, then remove with spatula to wire rack and cool completely. Store cookies in airtight container, or wrap tightly and freeze. *Makes about 100.*

FORMAL DINNER

EGGS WITH RUSSIAN
SAUCE*

STUFFED CROWN ROAST
OF LAMB*

WILD RICE AND
MUSHROOMS

SPINACH SALAD WITH
ORANGES*

PUMPKIN PIE A
L'ANGLAISE*

CHAMPAGNE OR DRY
WHITE SPARKLING WINE

RED BURGUNDY

For six.

WORK PLAN: Several hours before serving, do Step 1 of Eggs with Russian Sauce (below) and assemble all ingredients; finish dish just before serving. At the same time, soak apricots for Stuffed Crown Roast of Lamb and prepare Spinach Salad with Oranges (see page 30); assemble and dress salad at last moment.

Two hours before serving, prepare Stuffed Crown Roast of Lamb (page 30). Make Pumpkin Pie à l'Anglaise (page 30) and bake with lamb.

About 30 minutes before serving, cook 1½ cups wild rice or two 6-ounce packages brown and long-grain rice mix according to label directions, adding 1 cup sautéed sliced mushrooms just before serving.

Serve two kinds of wine with dinner.

EGGS WITH RUSSIAN SAUCE

1 cup mayonnaise
2½ tablespoons chili sauce
1 tablespoon chopped
    chives
1 tablespoon chopped
    parsley
1 teaspoon chopped green
    onion
2 drops hot pepper sauce
1 teaspoon lemon juice
½ teaspoon salt
¼ teaspoon Worcestershire
    sauce
6 lettuce leaves
6 hard-cooked eggs
small black olives, gherkins

1. Combine mayonnaise, chili sauce, chives, parsley, green onion, hot pepper sauce, lemon juice, salt and Worcestershire sauce. Cover and chill for several hours.

2. At serving time, place 1 lettuce leaf on each of 6 salad plates. Peel chilled eggs and cut lengthwise in half; place 2 halves flat side down on each plate. Cover eggs with sauce; garnish with small black olives and gherkins.

STUFFED CROWN ROAST OF LAMB

3 cups dried apricots
1 cup apple cider
½ cup dry vermouth
1 large onion, chopped
1 tablespoon brown sugar,
    firmly packed
crown roast of lamb using
    3 racks (about 6 or 7
    pounds), with ground
    lamb trimmings
salt and pepper to taste
rosemary

1. Soak apricots in mixture of cider and vermouth for several hours. Drain apricots, reserving liquid. Mix apricots with chopped onion; stir in brown sugar. Remove ground lamb from center of crown roast and stir it into the apricot mixture. Season with salt and pepper.

2. Sprinkle roast with salt, pepper and rosemary. Stuff center of roast with apricot-ground lamb mixture.

3. Place roast on wire rack in roasting pan. Roast lamb at 350° F for 2 hours or until meat thermometer reads 170° to 180° F and lamb is well done. During last hour of cooking, baste stuffing and crown roast every 15 minutes with reserved cider-vermouth mixture.

4. Slice roast into 2-rib sections and top each serving with some of the stuffing. *Pictured on the front cover.*

SPINACH SALAD WITH ORANGES

2 tablespoons lemon juice
2 teaspoons curry powder
1 teaspoon dry mustard
1 teaspoon salt
½ teaspoon Worcestershire
    sauce
½ teaspoon pepper
1 cup olive oil
1 clove garlic, crushed
one 10-ounce bag spinach
one 11-ounce can mandarin
    oranges, drained

1. In small bowl, mix lemon juice, curry, dry mustard, salt, Worcestershire sauce and pepper. Gradually add oil, stirring with fork or wire whisk. Place garlic in screwtop pint jar. Pour dressing into jar; cover and chill for several hours.

2. Wash spinach thoroughly. Drain and tear into bite-size pieces. Place in plastic bag; chill.

3. At serving time, place spinach in large salad bowl; add drained oranges. Shake dressing vigorously and pour about ⅓ cup over salad; toss to mix well. Reserve remaining dressing for later use.

PUMPKIN PIE A L'ANGLAISE

1 cup canned pumpkin
1 cup heavy cream
1 cup brown sugar, packed
3 eggs, slightly beaten
¼ cup dry sherry
1 teaspoon cinnamon
1 teaspoon nutmeg
1 teaspoon ginger
½ teaspoon salt
one 9-inch unbaked pastry
    pie shell
pouring cream

1. Preheat oven to 350° F.

2. In large bowl, mix pumpkin, heavy cream, brown sugar, slightly beaten eggs, sherry, cinnamon, nutmeg, ginger and salt.

3. Pour pumpkin mixture into unbaked pie shell. Bake for 60 to 70 minutes, until knife inserted in center comes out clean. Serve pie warm with pouring cream. *Makes one 9-inch pie.*

SUPPER PARTY

TOMATO-BEEF SOUP*

CREPES WITH HAM AND
CHEESE*

LEMON-BUTTERED
ASPARAGUS

MIXED GREEN SALAD

STRAWBERRY
SHERBET*

PECAN TARTS*

For six.

WORK PLAN: Several hours before serving, prepare Strawberry Sherbet and Pecan Tarts (page 33). At the same time, prepare Crêpes (page 32). If desired, make filling and sauce for Crêpes ahead of time and chill.

Forty-five minutes before serving, assemble and bake Crêpes with Ham and Cheese. For salad, combine 2 cups each watercress sprigs, bite-size pieces endive, and tiny Boston or Bibb and romaine lettuce leaves in large salad bowl; cover and chill. Toss with ½ cup bottled herb and spice vinaigrette dressing just before serving. Prepare Tomato-Beef Soup (below). Then rinse and trim 2 pounds fresh asparagus; simmer in large skillet in ½ inch water containing 1 teaspoon each salt and sugar. Drain, and toss with ¼ cup each butter or margarine and lemon juice. (Or similarly prepare three 10-ounce packages frozen asparagus spears.)

TOMATO-BEEF SOUP

two 10¾-ounce cans
  condensed tomato soup
two 10½-ounce cans
  condensed beef bouillon
1 cup thin onion rings
1 cup water
1 tablespoon lemon juice
6 whole black peppercorns
½ teaspoon salt
¼ teaspoon nutmeg
¼ cup dry sherry
1 tablespoon chopped
  parsley

1. In large saucepan, combine condensed tomato soup and beef bouillon, onion rings, water, lemon juice, peppercorns, salt and nutmeg. Quickly bring to boiling point; reduce heat to low and simmer, covered, for 30 minutes.

2. Strain soup; return to low heat and stir in sherry. Serve in bouillon cups or small soup bowls. Sprinkle with parsley before serving.

CREPES WITH HAM AND CHEESE

Crêpes (recipe below)

FILLING
½ cup butter or margarine
2 cups chopped onions
3 cups chopped mushrooms
6 cups chopped precooked
  ham (about 1½ pounds)
1½ teaspoons salt
½ teaspoon nutmeg
¼ teaspoon tarragon
¼ teaspoon pepper

SAUCE
⅓ cup butter or margarine
⅓ cup flour
4 cups milk
⅛ teaspoon cayenne pepper,
  or 2 to 3 drops hot pepper
  sauce
4 cups grated Swiss cheese

1. Prepare Crêpes. If made ahead of time, thaw and reheat. (Or keep warm while making filling and sauce.)

2. To make filling, melt ½ cup butter or margarine in large skillet over medium heat; add onions and sauté for 5 minutes, until soft and golden. Add mushrooms and sauté 5 minutes longer, stirring occasionally. Stir in ham, salt, nutmeg, tarragon and pepper; mix very well. Set aside.

3. To make sauce, melt ⅓ cup butter or margarine in medium saucepan over medium heat; blend in flour and cook for 2 to 3 minutes, stirring constantly. Gradually add milk, stirring with wire whisk to blend; add cayenne or hot pepper sauce. Bring to boiling point, stirring constantly; add 3 cups of the grated cheese, stirring until melted.

4. Preheat oven to 350° F.

5. To assemble crêpes, butter 6 individual ovenproof au gratin dishes; sprinkle 2 tablespoons ham mixture over bottom of each. Fill each crêpe with 2 to 3 tablespoons ham mixture. Roll crêpes jelly-roll fashion or fold into fourths to contain filling. Place 3 crêpes in each dish.

6. Pour ½ to ¾ cup sauce over each portion. Sprinkle with remaining 1 cup grated cheese. Bake for 25 to 30 minutes, until cheese is golden and sauce is bubbly.

Note: Filling and sauce can be prepared ahead of time, chilled and reheated before assembling crêpes.

Crêpes

1½ cups instant-blending
  flour
1 cup water
1 cup milk
4 large eggs, beaten
½ teaspoon salt
¼ cup butter or margarine,
  melted
vegetable oil

1. Place flour in large mixing bowl. Gradually stir in water and milk, then beaten eggs and salt. Pour in melted butter or margarine; mix well with wire whisk or fork.

2. Heat ½ teaspoon oil in 6-inch heavy iron crêpe pan or small skillet over medium heat. When very hot, pour in a scant ¼ cup batter; tilt skillet to cover surface completely and evenly. Cook for 1 minute; turn with metal spatula and cook second side for 30 seconds. Slide finished crêpe onto plate. Repeat with remaining batter. *Makes 24.*

Note: Crêpes can be made ahead of time. When cool, stack between layers of waxed paper and overwrap with foil. Freeze until ready to use, then thaw at room temperature for 10 to 15 minutes. Place in jelly-roll pan, cover with damp dish towel and reheat in 300° F oven.

STRAWBERRY SHERBET

**two 10-ounce packages
  frozen sweetened
  strawberries**
**2 tablespoons orange
  liqueur**
mint sprigs

1. Thaw strawberries just until soft. Puree in blender for 1 minute; pour into bowl and stir in liqueur.

2. Pour into ice cube tray; cover with waxed paper and freeze for several hours, until firm. Twenty minutes before dessert time, set sherbet in refrigerator to soften. Just before serving, scoop into 6 small stemmed dessert glasses; garnish with mint sprigs.

PECAN TARTS

PASTRY
**one 3-ounce package cream
  cheese, softened**
**½ cup butter or margarine,
  softened**
1 cup flour

FILLING
1 egg
**¾ cup brown sugar, firmly
  packed**
**1 tablespoon butter or
  margarine**
1 teaspoon vanilla extract
⅛ teaspoon salt
1 cup finely chopped pecans

1. To make pastry, thoroughly blend cream cheese and ½ cup butter or margarine in medium bowl; mix in flour. Wrap in waxed paper or plastic wrap and chill for several hours. Form into 24 balls and press into 1½-inch-wide tart pans.

2. Preheat oven to 325° F.

3. To make filling, use electric mixer at medium speed to mix egg, brown sugar, 1 tablespoon butter or margarine, the vanilla extract and salt until very smooth. Stir in chopped pecans.

4. Spoon filling into prepared tart shells. Bake for 25 to 30 minutes, until wooden toothpick inserted in center comes out clean. *Makes 24.*

Nothing brings something special to the final course of a dinner party like a rich and tender homemade pastry. The tart shells for the above recipe are mouthwatering even before they're filled! One secret of skillful pastry making is handling the dough as little as possible. If you wrap and chill it after mixing it, the dough will roll out quickly and easily, so the final product won't be tough.

WELCOME-SPRING DINNER

SHRIMP WITH PEPPER MAYONNAISE*

BROILED BONELESS LEG OF LAMB*

PARSLIED RICE

VEGETABLE SALAD*

ICE CREAM AND COOKIES

For six.

WORK PLAN: A day ahead of time, bone and marinate lamb (see recipe for Broiled Boneless Leg of Lamb, page 35).

Two or three hours before serving time, make Shrimp with Pepper Mayonnaise (below), combining shrimp and dressing just before serving. Similarly prepare Vegetable Salad (page 35). Drain lamb from marinade; broil as directed.

Twenty minutes before serving time, cook 1½ cups long-grain rice according to label directions; toss with ¼ cup chopped parsley before serving.

At dessert time, divide 1½ quarts mint chocolate chip ice cream among 6 dessert dishes; serve with chocolate-filled cookies.

SHRIMP WITH PEPPER MAYONNAISE

4 quarts water
1 tablespoon lemon juice
1 stalk celery, quartered
1 carrot, quartered
1 small onion, quartered
1 teaspoon salt
10 whole black peppercorns
1 pound large shrimp, washed

PEPPER MAYONNAISE
2 tablespoons vinegar
1 tablespoon lemon juice
1 egg
4 teaspoons green peppercorns
1 teaspoon salt
½ teaspoon prepared mustard
1½ cups vegetable oil

lettuce leaves

1. In large saucepan, combine water, 1 tablespoon lemon juice, the celery, carrot, onion, 1 teaspoon salt and the black peppercorns. Bring to boiling point and boil for 10 minutes.

2. Add unshelled shrimp to boiling water. Bring to boiling point again; remove shrimp and cool slightly. Shell and devein shrimp. Chill.

3. To make pepper mayonnaise, combine vinegar, 1 tablespoon lemon juice and the egg in electric blender. Add green peppercorns, 1 teaspoon salt and the mustard; process to blend. Slowly add oil to blender, processing at medium speed. Chill.

4. Serve shrimp on 6 lettuce-lined salad plates. Pour mayonnaise over shrimp or serve separately.

BROILED BONELESS LEG OF LAMB

6- to 7-pound whole leg of
  lamb (or 2 halves)
2 large onions, sliced
¾ cup olive or vegetable oil
¼ cup lemon juice
1 teaspoon salt
2 teaspoons chopped fresh
  rosemary, or 1 teaspoon
  dried rosemary
½ teaspoon pepper
2 large bay leaves
2 cloves garlic, sliced
1 tablespoon coarse salt
3 lemons, quartered

1. With sharp, narrow-bladed knife, bone lamb, cutting around bones as closely as possible; meat will look ragged. (Or ask your butcher to bone lamb.)

2. In large bowl, combine onions, oil, lemon juice, 1 teaspoon regular salt, the rosemary, pepper, bay leaves and garlic. Place lamb in marinade, turning to coat. Cover with plastic wrap and refrigerate overnight.

3. Remove meat from marinade 1 hour before grilling; reserve marinade. Prepare charcoal grill. Sprinkle meat with coarse salt.

4. Grill meat 4 inches from heat, 15 to 20 minutes per side. Baste with marinade when meat is turned. Slice lamb ¼ inch thick. Serve with lemon wedges.

VEGETABLE SALAD

1 green pepper, halved,
  seeded and thinly sliced
1 large Bermuda onion,
  thinly sliced
2 carrots, sliced
3 stalks celery, cut into
  2-inch pieces
2 tomatoes, peeled and
  sliced

DRESSING
1 cup vegetable oil
⅓ cup tarragon vinegar
¼ cup tomato sauce
1 tablespoon sugar
1 tablespoon chopped fresh
  basil, or 1 teaspoon
  crumbled dried basil
1 teaspoon Worcestershire
  sauce
1 teaspoon grated lemon
  rind
¼ teaspoon prepared
  mustard
¼ teaspoon salt
¼ teaspoon pepper
1 clove garlic, crushed

lettuce leaves (optional)

1. In large bowl, combine green pepper, onion, carrots, celery and tomatoes. Cover and refrigerate.

2. To make dressing, process oil, vinegar, tomato sauce, sugar, basil, Worcestershire sauce, lemon rind, mustard, salt, pepper and garlic in electric blender until well mixed; refrigerate until serving time.

3. Just before serving, stir dressing and pour over vegetables; toss to mix. Serve on lettuce leaves if desired.

SIT-DOWN DINNER

MARINATED SHRIMP*

ROAST CHICKEN

GREEN BEANS WITH
PARMESAN

ZUCCHINI TIMBALES*

HOT LEMON SOUFFLE*

For six.

WORK PLAN: Several hours ahead of time or the day before, prepare Marinated Shrimp (page 37).

Two hours before serving time, wash and dry a 4- to 5-pound roasting chicken or small capon; season well inside and out with salt and pepper. Stuff body cavity with 2 bunches washed parsley and 3 onions, cut into eighths; secure cavity with string or skewers. Place chicken on wire rack in roasting pan; pour ½ cup oil over chicken, and roast at 375° F for 1½ to 2 hours, basting frequently. Drumsticks should move freely and juices run clear when done.

About 30 minutes before serving time, prepare Zucchini Timbales (below), baking alongside chicken. Next, wash and trim 2 pounds fresh green beans; cook in boiling salted water to cover until just tender, about 8 minutes. Drain beans and keep warm; just before serving, toss with ¼ cup each butter or margarine and grated Parmesan cheese. Just before serving appetizer, prepare Hot Lemon Soufflé but do not bake (page 37). Let stand at room temperature in soufflé dish, covered with large mixing bowl. (Do not make soufflé mixture more than 30 minutes ahead of cooking time.) Place soufflé in oven when chicken is served.

ZUCCHINI TIMBALES

**2 cups grated zucchini
(about 1 pound)**
½ cup grated Swiss cheese
¼ cup finely chopped onion
**¼ cup dry seasoned bread
crumbs**
½ teaspoon salt
⅛ teaspoon pepper
3 eggs
3 tablespoons vegetable oil

1. Preheat oven to 375° F.

2. In large bowl, mix zucchini, cheese, onion, bread crumbs, salt and pepper. Beat in eggs.

3. Place 1 teaspoon oil in each of six 6-ounce custard cups or individual soufflé dishes. Heat in oven, then spoon zucchini mixture into cups. Bake for 18 to 20 minutes or until golden brown. Serve immediately.

MARINATED SHRIMP

30 large shrimp (about 2
   pounds), shelled and
   deveined
one 9-ounce can artichoke
   hearts, drained, or one
   10-ounce package frozen
   artichoke hearts, thawed
½ cup olive oil
½ cup peanut oil
¼ cup wine vinegar
2 tablespoons chopped
   parsley
2 tablespoons chopped
   chives
2 tablespoons chopped
   shallots
1 tablespoon lemon juice
1 tablespoon Dijon-style
   mustard
⅛ teaspoon salt
⅛ teaspoon pepper
Boston lettuce cups or
   watercress

1. Cook shrimp in boiling water to cover for about 5 minutes (do not overcook). Drain shrimp and combine with artichokes.

2. In large bowl, blend olive oil, peanut oil, vinegar, parsley, chives, shallots, lemon juice, mustard, salt and pepper. Add shrimp and artichokes; toss to coat well. Cover bowl with plastic wrap. Refrigerate for at least 4 hours or overnight. Stir several times while marinating.

3. To serve, remove shrimp and artichokes from marinade; reserve marinade. Place a Boston lettuce cup or bed of watercress on each of 6 salad plates; spoon shrimp and artichokes into cups. Pass reserved marinade as extra dressing.

HOT LEMON SOUFFLE

2 teaspoons unsalted butter
   or margarine
½ cup granulated sugar
3 tablespoons lemon juice
1 tablespoon grated lemon
   rind
4 egg yolks
6 egg whites

TOPPING
1 cup heavy cream
3 tablespoons confectioners'
   sugar
½ teaspoon vanilla extract

1. Preheat oven to 400° F. Grease 2-quart soufflé dish with unsalted butter or margarine. Sprinkle 2 tablespoons of the granulated sugar in dish; turn to coat sides and bottom, then shake out excess sugar.

2. Using electric mixer at high speed, beat egg yolks and remaining granulated sugar in large bowl until thick and lemon colored. Clean beaters very well. With mixer at high speed, beat egg whites in another large bowl until stiff peaks form. Fold one-fourth of egg whites into yolk mixture until well blended; gently fold in remaining whites just until blended. Pour into prepared soufflé dish. Bake for 10 to 12 minutes. Do not open oven until 2 minutes before end of cooking time.

3. Meanwhile, make topping by using electric mixer at high speed to beat cream until stiff. Slowly beat in 2 tablespoons of the confectioners' sugar and the vanilla extract. Sprinkle remaining confectioners' sugar on soufflé as it comes out of oven, and serve immediately with beaten cream alongside.

SEASIDE DINNER

CRUDITES

FISH SOUP*

HERB BREAD*

CHOCOLATE CAKE

For six.

WORK PLAN: Three hours before serving time, prepare Herb Bread (below). While bread is rising, mix and bake one 18.5-ounce package chocolate cake according to label directions; cool. Fill and frost with 2 cups chocolate buttercream (your own recipe or ready-to-spread frosting from one 16-ounce can). Cover sides and top of frosted cake with 1 cup grated chocolate.

About an hour and a half before serving time, prepare Fish Soup (page 39), and serve with warm Herb Bread. Prepare crudités by arranging about 1 cup each celery and carrot sticks, fresh radishes, cucumber and zucchini sticks, black and green olives, green pepper strips and broccoli and cauliflower sprigs on large platter; cover and chill. Prepare dipping sauce of 2 cups unflavored yogurt, 2 tablespoons dried dill and 2 teaspoons grated lemon rind; chill until serving time. (Crudités may be served as appetizer or as a salad accompaniment to the soup, with the yogurt dressing spooned over each portion.)

HERB BREAD

1 package active dry yeast
¼ cup very warm water
3 cups flour
2 tablespoons sugar
2 teaspoons salt
1 teaspoon caraway seeds
1 teaspoon powdered sage
1¼ cups lukewarm water
2 tablespoons butter or
    margarine, melted

1. Sprinkle yeast over ¼ cup very warm water (which feels comfortably warm when dropped on wrist) in large bowl; stir to dissolve.

2. Using electric mixer at medium speed, mix 1½ cups of the flour, the sugar, salt, caraway seeds and sage into yeast mixture. Add 1¼ cups lukewarm water and the melted butter or margarine. Beat mixture at high speed for 2 minutes.

3. Beat in remaining 1½ cups flour. Beat at high speed 2 minutes longer or until dough is shiny and elastic. Scrape down side of bowl; cover with clean towel. Let rise in warm, draft-free place for 1½ hours or until doubled in bulk.

4. Beat down dough; spread in greased 9 x 5 x 3-inch loaf pan. Cover with clean towel and let rise in warm, draft-free place for 30 minutes or until almost doubled in bulk.

5. Preheat oven to 400° F.

6. Bake bread for 40 to 45 minutes, until loaf is golden brown and sounds hollow when tapped. Cool in pan on wire rack for 10 minutes. Loosen around sides with long sharp knife; invert onto wire rack. *Makes 1 loaf.*

FISH SOUP

5 pounds fish bones, heads and tails
one 8-ounce bottle clam juice
4 large onions, sliced
2 carrots, sliced
2 stalks celery (with leaves), sliced
1½ cups chopped tomatoes (with juice)
juice of 1 lemon
1 clove garlic, halved
6 sprigs parsley
1 tablespoon salt
½ teaspoon black pepper
¼ teaspoon cayenne pepper
bay leaf
2¼ pounds boneless rock fish or other white fish, cubed
1 teaspoon saffron
1 cup cream
2 tablespoons butter or margarine
2 tablespoons flour
2 cups coarsely chopped mushrooms
croutons

1. In very large saucepan, combine fish bones, heads and tails with clam juice, onions, carrots, celery, tomatoes, lemon juice, garlic, parsley, salt, black pepper, cayenne and bay leaf. Simmer, partially covered, for 1 hour.

2. Strain through sieve, pressing down with spoon to remove all juices. Return liquid to saucepan. Add cubed fish; simmer gently over low heat for 10 to 15 minutes, just until fish flakes. Remove fish from saucepan. Skin if necessary and set aside.

3. In small bowl, combine 1 cup of the hot fish broth with saffron. Return mixture to saucepan. Add cream; stir to mix well.

4. In small bowl, combine butter or margarine and flour. Stir into soup. Cook for 5 minutes or until thickened.

5. Return fish to soup. Add mushrooms. Simmer for 5 to 10 minutes, until fish is hot and mushrooms are tender. Serve in hot soup bowls. Top with croutons.

Note: This soup serves six generously; cool and freeze surplus for later use.

SATURDAY NIGHT DINNER PARTY

SMOKED SALMON

BOILED BEEF WITH MUSTARD SAUCE*

HOT FRENCH BREAD

BIBB LETTUCE-AVOCADO SALAD

FRESH FRUIT AND POUND CAKE*

For eight.

WORK PLAN: Two hours before serving time, prepare Pound Cake (page 41); serve in slices with chilled fresh fruit.

One hour before serving time, prepare Boiled Beef with Mustard Sauce (below). At the same time, arrange 2 or 3 slices smoked salmon on each of 8 small serving plates; garnish with chopped hard-cooked egg, capers, lemon wedges, freshly ground pepper and sliced brown bread. Chill until ready to serve.

Thirty minutes before serving time, arrange 1 head Bibb lettuce, cut into fourths, and 6 to 8 slices avocado on each of 8 salad plates; chill until serving time, then dress with olive oil and tarragon vinegar.

About 15 minutes before serving time, cut French bread loaf into ½-inch slices to within ¼ inch of bottom; spread slices with mixture of ½ cup butter or margarine, softened, ¼ cup grated Parmesan cheese and 1 clove garlic, crushed. Wrap in foil and heat for 10 minutes in 350° F oven. *Pictured on page 49.*

BOILED BEEF WITH MUSTARD SAUCE

6- to 7-pound beef fillet, at room temperature
3 quarts water
1 pound carrots, peeled and cut into eighths
1 pound turnips, peeled and cut into eighths
1 bunch celery, trimmed and cut into eighths
10 small onions, peeled
2 tablespoons chopped fresh tarragon
1 tablespoon salt
10 peppercorns
3 marrow bones
Mustard Sauce (page 41)
sour pickles, pickled onions

1. Trim off and discard narrow end and most of fat from fillet. Tie fillet with butcher's twine so that it will keep its shape. Make a loop at each end of meat to facilitate removal from pan.

2. In large saucepan, combine water, carrots, turnips, celery, onions, tarragon, salt, peppercorns and marrow bones. Bring to boiling point; boil for 5 minutes.

3. Add meat, hanging loop of string over edge of pan. Bring to boiling point again; reduce heat to low and simmer for 35 to 50 minutes, skimming surface frequently. After 35 minutes, slice one end of meat to test degree of doneness.

4. Meanwhile, make Mustard Sauce. Remove cooked meat to warm platter. Using slotted spoon, remove vegetables from pan and arrange around meat. Pour ½ cup of the cooking broth over meat and vegetables; strain remaining broth and store for use in soup. Accompany meat and vegetables with small sour pickles, small pickled onions and Mustard Sauce.

Note: An economic substitute for fillet of beef is eye of round. Tenderize it with instant meat tenderizer before fixing it as above.

Mustard Sauce

2 egg yolks
1½ tablespoons vinegar
1 tablespoon dry mustard
½ teaspoon salt
¼ teaspoon pepper
1½ cups vegetable oil

1. Using electric mixer at high speed, beat egg yolks in small bowl until thick and lemon colored. Beat in vinegar, dry mustard, salt and pepper.

2. Add oil, drop by drop, then in thin stream. Beat at medium-high speed until yolks and oil are thoroughly combined. Chill until serving time. *Makes about 2 cups.*

POUND CAKE

CAKE
one 18.5-ounce package
** yellow cake mix**
1 cup sour cream
¾ cup vegetable oil
½ cup granulated sugar
½ teaspoon vanilla extract
¼ teaspoon almond extract
4 eggs

FILLING
3 tablespoons brown sugar
1 tablespoon cinnamon

GLAZE
2 cups confectioners' sugar
½ teaspoon vanilla extract
⅓ to ½ cup heavy cream

1. Preheat oven to 325° F. Grease and flour 10-inch fluted or plain tube pan.

2. To make cake, combine cake mix, sour cream, oil, granulated sugar, ½ teaspoon vanilla extract and the almond extract in large bowl. Add eggs one at a time, beating well after each addition. Pour half of batter into prepared pan.

3. To make filling, combine brown sugar and cinnamon in small bowl. Distribute evenly over cake batter in pan. Pour remaining batter on top of filling.

4. Bake for 45 to 50 minutes, until cake tester inserted in center comes out clean. Cool in pan on wire rack for 10 minutes. Loosen around side and tube with long sharp knife; invert cake onto wire rack to cool completely.

5. To make glaze, place confectioners' sugar in small bowl; add ½ teaspoon vanilla extract and enough cream to produce glaze of spreading consistency. Spread glaze over cooled cake. *Makes one 10-inch tube cake.*

Brunches and Buffets

If you love to entertain but haven't the time or inclination to put together a dinner party, consider throwing a casual, spur-of-the-moment brunch or a stunning buffet party. Your guests will wish they'd thought of it first!

Sunday brunch has practically become an institution. For most busy people, Sunday is the one luxurious day of the week to forget about jobs, errands and at-home chores. But it's also the perfect day for easy, spontaneous visiting and chatting. Even when you're playing host or hostess, you can keep your morning leisurely by making one big dish the day before—perhaps a dessert like moist, nutty Carrot Cake, an elaborate salad like the molded Black Raspberry-Grapefruit-Cherry Salad, or a savory filling such as the hale and hearty one for the Veal and Pork Pies. That way, preparation time will be kept to a minimum.

For a really big gathering, nothing beats a buffet. The whole menu—desserts included—can be set out all at once. Some hot dishes, some cold dishes, but all of them "help-yourself" dishes give your party a free and easy air. These buffet party menus will serve eight to twelve party-goers, yet most require no more than $4^{1}/_{2}$ hours of pre-party preparation. If your style—by choice or necessity—is "do-ahead," you're in luck. Mouthwatering creations like Crisp Chicken Kiev, Feta-Spinach Turnovers and fresh Coconut Cake can be made anywhere from a day to a week beforehand, then refrigerated or frozen. On the day of your party, you can concentrate on being the perfect host or hostess —your cooking chores are behind you.

So break out of the mold. Throw a brunch or buffet bash—at your leisure.

AUTUMN BRUNCH

GLAZED GRAPEFRUIT

EGG-BACON-CHEESE STRATA*

HOT TEA WITH CIDER*

For six.

WORK PLAN: About 45 minutes before serving, prepare Egg-Bacon-Cheese Strata (below). To make glazed grapefruit, halve and section 3 pink grapefruit; sprinkle each half with 1 tablespoon brown sugar. Broil 6 inches from heat for 3 to 4 minutes. Prepare Hot Tea with Cider (below).

EGG-BACON-CHEESE STRATA

6 slices whole wheat bread
6 slices sharp Cheddar cheese
6 eggs, well beaten
2 cups milk
½ teaspoon salt
½ teaspoon pepper
12 slices bacon, crisply fried and drained
2 tablespoons butter or margarine
1 tablespoon parsley flakes

1. Preheat oven to 350° F.

2. Trim crusts from bread; reserve crusts. Line bottom of greased 12 x 8 x 2-inch baking dish with trimmed bread slices. Top with cheese slices.

3. Combine beaten eggs and milk; add salt and pepper. Pour over bread and cheese. Crumble bacon on top of mixture.

4. In electric blender, process reserved crusts to make bread crumbs. Melt butter or margarine in medium skillet over medium heat; add crumbs and sauté until butter or margarine is absorbed. Add parsley. Sprinkle crumb mixture over egg-bacon mixture.

5. Bake for 25 minutes. Increase heat to 400° F and bake 5 minutes longer or until puffy, golden brown and firm. Let stand for 5 minutes before serving.

HOT TEA WITH CIDER

1½ cups unsweetened apple cider, heated
2 tablespoons brown sugar
4½ cups hot brewed tea

In large heatproof pitcher, add cider and brown sugar to hot tea. (Or, for each serving, add ¼ cup apple cider and 1 teaspoon brown sugar to ¾ cup tea.)

PRE-GAME BRUNCH

MEAT ROLL-UP WITH
TOMATO SAUCE*

CRISP GREEN SALAD

MERINGUE CAKE*

COFFEE

For eight.

WORK PLAN: A day ahead of time, prepare Meringue Cake (page 45). Fill and frost cake just before serving.

One hour before serving, prepare Meat Roll-Up with Tomato Sauce (below). While it cooks, make green salad by combining 6 cups torn leafy salad greens in large bowl; cover and chill. Just before serving, toss with 1 cup crisp croutons and ½ cup red wine salad dressing.

Serve hot coffee with brunch.

MEAT ROLL-UP WITH TOMATO SAUCE

ROLL-UP
1½ cups flour
½ cup cornmeal
2½ teaspoons salt
½ cup butter or margarine
½ cup milk
1 pound lean ground beef
½ cup chopped onion
½ cup oatmeal
⅔ cup vegetable juice
1 egg, beaten
¼ teaspoon pepper

SAUCE
one 15-ounce can tomato
  sauce
½ cup diced celery
½ cup water
2 tablespoons brown sugar
1 tablespoon lemon juice
¼ teaspoon dry mustard
¼ teaspoon pepper

1. Preheat oven to 425° F.

2. To make roll-up, combine flour, cornmeal and 1 teaspoon of the salt in medium bowl. Using two knives or a pastry blender, cut in butter or margarine until mixture resembles coarse cornmeal. Using fork, stir in milk just until dough leaves sides of bowl. Knead lightly in bowl just until dough holds together and is smooth. Roll out on waxed paper to 12 x 9-inch rectangle.

3. In medium bowl, combine ground beef, onion, oatmeal, vegetable juice, beaten egg, remaining 1½ teaspoons salt and ¼ teaspoon pepper until just blended. Pat onto crust to within ½ inch of edges of crust. Starting at long end, roll up jelly-roll fashion. Place seam side down on large ungreased baking sheet. Bake for 15 minutes; reduce heat to 325° F and bake 30 minutes longer.

4. Meanwhile, make sauce by combining tomato sauce, celery, water, brown sugar, lemon juice, dry mustard and ¼ teaspoon pepper in medium saucepan. Simmer for 15 minutes or until celery is tender.

5. To serve, cut roll-up into 2-inch slices; place on heated serving platter. Pour part of sauce over slices; pass remaining sauce.

Note: This dish can be made ahead and frozen. Bake roll-up and simmer sauce as directed; wrap separately and freeze. Thaw both at room temperature for 3 hours or in refrigerator overnight. Reheat roll-up at 325° F for 30 minutes and simmer sauce for 5 minutes, until heated through.

MERINGUE CAKE

1 cup cake flour
2 teaspoons baking powder
½ teaspoon salt
½ cup butter or margarine
½ cup granulated sugar
4 egg yolks
5 tablespoons milk
1 teaspoon vanilla extract

CHOCOLATE LAYER
one 6-ounce package
  semisweet chocolate
  morsels
2 tablespoons crème de
  cacao
2 tablespoons butter or
  margarine

MERINGUE LAYER
4 egg whites
1 cup granulated sugar
½ cup chopped pecans
¼ cup graham cracker
  crumbs

CHOCOLATE WHIPPED
  CREAM
1 cup heavy cream
2 tablespoons crème de
  cacao
1 tablespoon confectioners'
  sugar

1. Preheat oven to 350° F. Sift flour, baking powder and salt onto waxed paper; set aside.

2. Using electric mixer at high speed, beat ½ cup butter or margarine and ½ cup granulated sugar in large bowl. Add yolks one at a time, beating after each addition.

3. Combine milk and vanilla extract in 1-cup measure. With mixer at low speed, add sifted dry ingredients alternately with milk mixture to butter-egg mixture; mix just until well blended. Spread batter in 2 well-greased 8-inch cake pans.

4. To make chocolate layer, combine chocolate morsels, 2 tablespoons crème de cacao and 2 tablespoons butter or margarine in medium saucepan. Heat over low heat, stirring constantly, until chocolate is melted. Using rubber spatula, spread over batter in pans while still warm.

5. To make meringue layer, use electric mixer at high speed to beat egg whites in small bowl until foamy-white and doubled in volume. Add 1 cup granulated sugar, 1 tablespoon at a time, until stiff peaks form. Fold pecans and cracker crumbs into meringue; spread over chocolate layer in cake pans.

6. Bake for 25 minutes or until meringue is golden and wooden toothpick inserted in center comes out clean. Cool in pans on wire rack for 10 minutes. Loosen layers around edges of pans with small spatula. Invert each layer onto a plate and immediately turn meringue side up. Cool completely. Store overnight in airtight plastic container.

7. Just before serving, make chocolate whipped cream by using electric mixer at high speed to beat cream in small bowl until stiff; fold in 2 tablespoons crème de cacao and the confectioners' sugar. Use whipped cream to fill and frost cake. *Makes one 8-inch layer cake.*

GOURMET BRUNCH

CHICKEN AND DRIED
BEEF IN WINE*

SPINACH RING*

SPICED PEACHES*

MINCE TARTS WITH
APPLEJACK HARD
SAUCE*

COFFEE

For eight.

WORK PLAN: A day ahead of time, prepare Spiced Peaches and Mince Tarts with Applejack Hard Sauce (page 48); the next day, reheat as directed. Make Rich Pastry Dough for Spinach Ring (page 47).

About 3½ hours before serving, prepare Chicken and Dried Beef in Wine (below). About 1¼ hours before serving, make pastry container for Spinach Ring; while it cools, prepare filling and proceed as directed (see page 47). Brew coffee while Spinach Ring bakes.

CHICKEN AND DRIED BEEF IN WINE

one 4-ounce jar dried beef
4 whole chicken breasts
⅓ cup flour
½ teaspoon salt
½ teaspoon white pepper
½ teaspoon paprika
¼ teaspoon marjoram
¼ teaspoon thyme
1 cup dry white wine
one 6-ounce can button
  mushrooms
2 tablespoons butter or
  margarine
¼ cup chopped parsley

1. Line greased 12 x 8 x 2-inch glass baking dish with dried beef.

2. Cut bones from chicken breasts with very sharp knife. Cut each breast lengthwise in half. Pound gently with smooth side of wooden mallet. Combine flour, salt, pepper, paprika, marjoram and thyme on waxed paper; coat chicken breasts with mixture. Shape each breast into neat serving. Place over dried beef in baking dish.

3. Pour wine over chicken; top with undrained mushrooms. Top with butter or margarine, cut into small slivers. Sprinkle with parsley. Cover baking dish with heavy-duty aluminum foil.

4. Bake at 250° F for 2 hours and 50 minutes. Remove foil from baking dish and increase temperature to 375° F. Bake 15 minutes longer or until chicken is brown.

SPINACH RING

Rich Pastry Dough (recipe below)

FILLING
one 10-ounce package frozen chopped spinach, thawed
1 tablespoon butter or margarine
½ cup finely chopped onion
6 eggs, separated
1 cup grated sharp Cheddar cheese
1 cup grated Parmesan cheese
one 8-ounce jar dried beef
1 tablespoon flour
½ teaspoon salt
1½ cups milk
1 teaspoon Dijon-style mustard

1. Make Rich Pastry Dough and chill as directed.

2. Preheat oven to 400° F. Grease outside of 8-cup ring mold.

3. Roll out pastry dough to ¼-inch thickness on lightly floured board. Cut into 14-inch round. Place on outside of ring mold; prick dough with fork. Place inverted ring mold on large baking sheet. Bake for 12 to 15 minutes, until pastry is light brown. Cool on wire rack for 10 minutes. Lower oven temperature to 350° F.

4. To make filling, drain thawed spinach very well by pressing in sieve; set aside. Melt butter or margarine in small skillet over medium heat; add onion and sauté until soft, about 5 minutes.

5. In electric blender, process spinach, sautéed onion, egg yolks, Cheddar and Parmesan cheeses, dried beef, flour, salt, milk and mustard at high speed until very smooth. Pour mixture into medium saucepan. Cook over low heat, stirring constantly, until mixture thickens. Remove from heat and cool for 10 minutes.

6. Using electric mixer at high speed, beat egg whites in large bowl until stiff. Using rubber spatula, fold into cooled spinach mixture just until blended.

7. Loosen pastry shell from ring mold with sharp knife and place on baking sheet. Fill with spinach mixture. Bake for 35 minutes or until soufflé is puffy and firm. Serve immediately.

Rich Pastry Dough

2 cups flour
1 teaspoon salt
½ cup vegetable shortening
¼ cup butter or margarine
5 tablespoons ice water

1. In medium bowl, combine flour and salt. Using two knives or a pastry blender, cut in shortening and butter or margarine until mixture resembles cornmeal.

2. Sprinkle mixture with ice water and toss with fork until dough leaves edge of bowl and forms a ball. Wrap in plastic wrap and chill overnight. *Makes enough for Spinach Ring (above), or one 2-crust pie.*

SPICED PEACHES

two 29-ounce cans peaches
⅔ cup vinegar
⅔ cup sugar
1 tablespoon pickling spices

1. Drain liquid from peaches; reserve ⅔ cup liquid and set peaches aside. Pour reserved liquid into medium saucepan. Add vinegar, sugar and pickling spices. Bring to boiling point and boil for 3 minutes. Remove from heat. Place drained peaches in hot syrup; let stand overnight.

2. The next day, bring peaches and syrup to rapid boil; immediately remove from heat. Let peaches cool in syrup until ready to serve.

MINCE TARTS WITH APPLEJACK HARD SAUCE

Rich Pastry Dough (page 47)
one 28-ounce jar mincemeat
   with brandy and rum
2 Winesap apples, peeled,
   cored and chopped
½ cup currants or raisins
Applejack Hard Sauce
   (recipe below)

1. Make Rich Pastry Dough; wrap in plastic wrap and chill in freezer for 30 minutes. Five minutes before rolling out dough, preheat oven to 425° F.

2. In medium bowl, combine mincemeat, apples and currants or raisins.

3. Roll out dough to ⅛-inch thickness on floured board. Using 3-inch cookie cutter, cut pastry dough to line sixteen 2½-inch muffin tins. Place dough in tins; fill each two-thirds full with mincemeat mixture.

4. Bake for 30 minutes or until pastry is golden. Serve hot with Applejack Hard Sauce.

Note: These tarts can be made ahead, wrapped in foil and reheated at 325° F for 15 minutes.

Applejack Hard Sauce

½ cup butter
2 cups confectioners' sugar
3 tablespoons applejack or
   Calvados brandy

In small bowl, beat butter until soft. Blend in confectioners' sugar and applejack or brandy until smooth. Serve on Mince Tarts. *Makes about 1½ cups.*

Note: Use only butter in this very traditional recipe. The sauce can be used to accompany Christmas pudding, Chrismas cake or any other steamed or baked pudding that is served with a hard sauce.

Saturday Night Dinner Party (*pages 40 and 41*)

Informal Dinner (*pages 18 and 19*)

Public House Brunch (*pages 56 and 57*)

Strawberry Torte (*page 136*)

Simple Sunday Brunch

SPINACH AND SAUSAGE
QUICHE*

RELISH TRAY

FRESH FRUIT CUP

COFFEE OR TEA

For eight.

WORK PLAN: One hour and 15 minutes before serving, prepare Spinach and Sausage Quiche (below). While quiche bakes, combine 3 grapefruit, peeled and sectioned, 3 dessert apples, cored and thinly sliced, 3 oranges, peeled and sectioned, and 1 pound green seedless grapes, halved, in large bowl; divide among 8 dessert dishes and chill until serving time. To prepare relish tray, arrange the 2 cups each 3-inch celery and carrot sticks, one 12-ounce jar each black and green olives, drained, and one 8-ounce jar gherkins, drained, on large platter; chill until serving time.

Offer choice of coffee or tea.

Spinach and Sausage Quiche

1 pound bulk sausage meat
½ cup thinly sliced onion
2 unbaked 8-inch pie shells
½ pound thinly sliced Swiss cheese
one 10-ounce package frozen chopped spinach, thawed and very well drained
6 eggs
3 cups light cream or half-and-half
1 teaspoon Dijon-style mustard
1 teaspoon crumbled basil
1 teaspoon crumbled tarragon
¾ teaspoon salt
½ teaspoon white pepper
⅛ teaspoon cayenne pepper

1. Preheat oven to 375° F.

2. Flatten sausage meat into large patty in large skillet. Brown on one side over medium heat; turn and brown on second side. Remove from skillet and crumble onto paper towels.

3. Drain all but 2 tablespoons drippings from skillet; add onion to drippings in skillet and sauté until soft, about 4 minutes.

4. Line pie shells with cheese, then add sausage and onion. Add drained spinach.

5. Using wire whisk, beat eggs in medium bowl; add cream or half-and-half, mustard, basil, tarragon, salt, white pepper and cayenne and beat until smooth. Slowly pour into pie shells.

6. Bake for about 40 minutes or until center is almost set but still soft. (Do not overbake; custard firms up as it cools.) Cool on wire rack for 15 minutes before serving. *Makes two 8-inch quiches.*

DOWN-HOME BRUNCH

CHICKEN AND BISCUITS*

APRICOT AND ORANGE FRUIT MOLD*

CARROT CAKE*

COFFEE OR TEA

For eight.

WORK PLAN: A day ahead of time, prepare Apricot and Orange Fruit Mold and Carrot Cake (page 55).

One hour before serving, make Chicken and Biscuits (below).

Serve hot coffee or tea with brunch.

CHICKEN AND BISCUITS

4 whole chicken breasts
1 onion, sliced
salt and pepper to taste
3 cups chopped carrots
1 cup chopped celery
one 10-ounce package
    frozen peas
3 tablespoons butter or
    margarine
3 tablespoons flour
1½ cups half-and-half or
    light cream
2 cups packaged biscuit mix

1. Using very sharp knife, skin and bone chicken breasts; cut breasts in half.

2. In large skillet, combine chicken breasts, onion, salt and pepper; add water to depth of ½ inch. Bring to boiling point; reduce heat to low and cover skillet. Simmer for 10 to 15 minutes, until chicken breasts are tender when pierced with two-tined fork. Remove chicken from skillet and cool; reserve 1½ cups of the chicken broth. Cut cooled chicken into bite-size pieces; set aside.

3. Steam carrots, celery and peas in medium saucepan for 5 minutes or until crisp-tender.

4. Melt butter or margarine in small saucepan over medium heat; add flour and stir until well blended. Slowly add half-and-half or cream and reserved chicken broth. Cook, stirring constantly, until mixture thickens and bubbles, about 3 minutes. Pour into 2-quart baking dish; add chicken and vegetables.

5. Preheat oven to 375° F.

6. Prepare biscuit mix according to label directions. Cut dough into 2½-inch rounds and arrange on top of chicken mixture. Bake for 15 minutes or until biscuits are golden and chicken is bubbly.

APRICOT AND ORANGE FRUIT MOLD

one 6-ounce package
   apricot-flavored gelatin
1 cup boiling water
1 cup orange juice
3 ice cubes
one 20-ounce can fruit
   cocktail, drained
1 cup unflavored yogurt

TOPPING
⅓ cup unflavored yogurt
1 tablespoon orange liqueur

1. In medium bowl, dissolve gelatin in boiling water; stir in orange juice and ice cubes. Refrigerate until mixture is consistency of unbeaten egg whites, about 20 minutes.

2. Pour ½ cup of the syrupy gelatin into 4-cup ring mold; refrigerate gelatin in mold and remaining gelatin until gelatin in mold is semi-set, about 20 minutes.

3. Fold drained fruit cocktail and 1 cup yogurt into remaining gelatin. Pour over bottom layer. Chill for at least 1½ to 2 hours or overnight, until set.

4. To unmold, loosen mold around edges with small sharp knife; quickly dip mold into hot water. Invert onto moistened serving plate and carefully shake to release.

5. To make topping, combine ⅓ cup yogurt and the orange liqueur in small bowl; serve alongside gelatin mold.

CARROT CAKE

4 eggs
2 cups sugar
two 7½-ounce jars baby food
   carrots
1½ cups vegetable oil
1 teaspoon vanilla extract
2 cups flour
2 teaspoons baking soda
1 teaspoon salt
1 teaspoon cinnamon
¼ teaspoon nutmeg
one 13¼-ounce can
   pineapple chunks, drained
1 cup chopped pecans
1 cup currants or raisins

1. Preheat oven to 350° F. Grease and flour 10-inch fluted or plain tube pan.

2. Using electric mixer at high speed, beat eggs in large bowl for 3 minutes. With mixer at medium speed, gradually beat in sugar, then carrots, oil and vanilla extract.

3. Sift flour, baking soda, salt, cinnamon and nutmeg into egg mixture; with mixer at low speed, blend well. Fold in drained pineapple, pecans and currants or raisins. Spoon into prepared pan.

4. Bake for 55 minutes or until cake tester inserted in center comes out clean. Cool in pan on wire rack for 1 hour. Loosen around edge and tube with long sharp knife. Invert cake onto wire rack to cool completely. *Makes one 10-inch tube cake.*

PUBLIC HOUSE BRUNCH

VEAL AND PORK PIES*

CITRUS SALAD*

CELERY STUFFED WITH CREAM CHEESE

EASY CHOCOLATE MOUSSE*

COFFEE OR TEA

For eight.

WORK PLAN: A day before serving, prepare filling for Veal and Pork Pies (below). Cool filling and refrigerate overnight. Make Citrus Salad (page 57); make topping just before serving the next day.

Two hours before serving, prepare Easy Chocolate Mousse (page 57). Make Lard Piecrust and bake Veal and Pork Pies (see recipe below). While pies bake, beat two 8-ounce packages cream cheese with ½ cup finely chopped pickles. Use to fill 12 large celery stalks; cut each into 3-inch pieces.

Serve coffee or tea with brunch.
Pictured on page 51.

VEAL AND PORK PIES

2 tablespoons vegetable oil
½ cup chopped onion
1 pound boneless veal shoulder, cut into ½-inch cubes
1 pound lean ground pork
3 cups water
3 cups diced peeled potatoes
2 cups sliced peeled carrots
1 teaspoon crumbled basil
1 teaspoon parsley flakes
½ teaspoon freshly ground pepper
½ teaspoon sage
½ teaspoon salt
2 tablespoons flour
Lard Piecrust (page 57)
1 egg, beaten

1. Heat oil in large saucepan over medium-high heat; add onion and sauté for 4 minutes, until golden. Add veal and pork and cook until brown, stirring frequently.

2. Add water. Simmer until liquid is reduced to 2 cups; reduce heat to low. Add potatoes, carrots, basil, parsley, pepper, sage and salt. Cook, covered, just until vegetables and veal are fork-tender, about 30 to 45 minutes.

3. Mix flour with a little water in 1-cup measure; stir into mixture in saucepan. Cook over medium heat, stirring gently, until mixture thickens and bubbles, about 3 minutes. Cool mixture completely; cover and chill overnight if desired.

4. Prepare Lard Piecrust. Divide dough into 4 balls. Roll out 2 balls on lightly floured cloth or board to ⅛-inch thickness; use to line two 8-inch pie plates. Spoon meat filling into pastry-lined pie plates. Roll out remaining 2 pastry balls to circles 2 inches larger than pie plate.

5. Cut one 2-inch circle from center of each to let steam escape; cover pie. Trim overhang to 1 inch; turn under, flush with rim, and flute. Brush both pies with beaten egg. Bake for 40 minutes or until pastry is golden. *Makes two 8-inch pies.*

Lard Piecrust

3 cups flour
1½ teaspoons salt
⅔ cup lard
⅓ to ½ cup ice water

1. In medium bowl, combine flour and salt. Using two knives or a pastry blender, cut in lard until mixture resembles cornmeal.

2. Add ice water, 1 tablespoon at a time, tossing with fork until pastry clings together and leaves side of bowl. *Makes enough for two 8-inch 2-crust pies.*

CITRUS SALAD

one 6-ounce package lemon-
**   flavored gelatin**
2 cups boiling water
1 cup cold water
½ cup orange or lemon juice
2 large pink grapefruit,
**   peeled and sectioned**
3 oranges, peeled and
**   sectioned**
1 cup seedless grapes

TOPPING
¼ cup mayonnaise
¼ cup sour cream

1. In deep medium-size bowl, dissolve gelatin in boiling water; stir in cold water and orange or lemon juice. Pour into 6-cup crystal bowl. Freeze for 15 minutes or until syrupy.

2. Add grapefruit, oranges and grapes to syrupy gelatin. Refrigerate for at least 4 hours or overnight.

3. Just before serving, make topping by combining mayonnaise with sour cream in small bowl. Spoon over gelatin.

EASY CHOCOLATE MOUSSE

one 12-ounce package
**   semisweet chocolate**
**   morsels**
½ cup sugar
6 eggs, separated
1 cup heavy cream

1. Melt chocolate in top of double boiler over simmering water. Stir in sugar.

2. Beat egg yolks; stir into chocolate mixture. Heat for 2 to 3 minutes, stirring constantly. Remove from heat.

3. Using electric mixer at high speed, beat cream in medium bowl until stiff; set aside. Clean beaters well. Using mixer at high speed, beat egg whites in another medium bowl until stiff. Fold beaten cream and egg whites into chocolate mixture.

4. Divide mixture among 8 individual soufflé dishes or 10-ounce custard cups. Chill until serving time.

PRIMAVERA BRUNCH

SHRIMP CASSEROLE ON TOAST*

BLACK RASPBERRY-GRAPEFRUIT-CHERRY SALAD*

ASPARAGUS WITH BLUE CHEESE-SESAME DRESSING*

MOCHA BROWNIES* AND ICE CREAM

COFFEE OR TEA

For eight.

WORK PLAN: A day ahead of time, prepare Black Raspberry-Grapefruit-Cherry Salad (page 59). Prepare Mocha Brownies (page 59); serve the next day with 1½ quarts coffee ice cream scooped on top.

Forty-five minutes before serving, make Shrimp Casserole on Toast (below). While casserole bakes, prepare Asparagus with Blue Cheese-Sesame Dressing (page 59).

Make coffee or tea to serve with brunch.

SHRIMP CASSEROLE ON TOAST

2 pounds fresh shrimp, shelled and deveined
½ cup water
½ cup dry white wine
⅓ cup butter or margarine
⅓ cup flour
2 cups milk
1 cup light cream or half-and-half
½ cup dry sherry
1 teaspoon salt
½ teaspoon white pepper
2 tablespoons butter or margarine
1 cup sliced mushrooms
¼ cup chopped onion
½ cup grated Parmesan cheese
8 slices whole wheat toast, buttered and quartered

1. In medium saucepan, cook shrimp in mixture of simmering water and wine for 3 to 5 minutes, just until shrimp turn pink; drain shrimp from pan and set aside. Pour liquid from pan; reserve for another use.

2. Melt ⅓ cup butter or margarine in same saucepan over medium heat; blend in flour and cook, stirring constantly, until bubbly. Slowly stir in milk, cream or half-and-half, sherry, salt and pepper. Cook, stirring frequently, until mixture thickens. Remove from heat.

3. Melt 2 tablespoons butter or margarine in small saucepan over medium heat; add mushrooms and onion and sauté until tender, about 5 minutes.

4. Stir shrimp into cream sauce; add mushrooms and onions. Place in greased 2-quart casserole; top with grated cheese. Bake at 350° F for 25 minutes or until bubbly and light golden brown; serve over buttered toast points.

BLACK RASPBERRY-GRAPEFRUIT-CHERRY SALAD

one 6-ounce package black
   raspberry-flavored gelatin
1½ cups boiling water
9 ice cubes
one 16-ounce jar grapefruit
   sections, drained
one 8-ounce container black
   cherry yogurt

1. In medium bowl, dissolve gelatin in boiling water. Add ice cubes; stir until dissolved. Pour ½ cup of the gelatin into 3½-cup ring mold. Refrigerate mold and remaining gelatin until gelatin in mold is semi-set, about 20 minutes.

2. Place drained grapefruit sections over gelatin in mold. Stir yogurt into remaining gelatin and spoon over grapefruit. Refrigerate until firm, at least 2 hours or overnight.

3. To unmold, loosen mold around edges with knife; quickly dip mold into hot water. Invert onto moistened serving platter and carefully shake to release mold.

ASPARAGUS WITH BLUE CHEESE-SESAME DRESSING

2 pounds fresh asparagus,
   or three 10-ounce
   packages frozen
   asparagus spears
1 cup water
2 teaspoons salt
2 teaspoons sugar

DRESSING
¾ cup bottled blue cheese
   salad dressing
2 tablespoons sour cream
2 tablespoons toasted
   sesame seeds

1. Wash fresh asparagus and break off tough ends. Place asparagus in large skillet with water, salt and sugar. Cover and simmer over medium heat for 5 minutes or until crisp-tender. (Or prepare frozen asparagus according to label directions, adding salt and sugar to cooking water.)

2. To make dressing, combine blue cheese dressing, sour cream and sesame seeds in small bowl. Serve dressing over asparagus.

MOCHA BROWNIES

1⅓ cups flour
1¼ teaspoons baking
   powder
1 teaspoon salt
¾ cup butter or margarine
four 1-ounce squares
   unsweetened chocolate
1 teaspoon instant coffee
   powder
4 eggs
2 cups sugar
1½ teaspoons vanilla extract
1 cup chopped walnuts

1. Preheat oven to 350° F. Sift flour, baking powder and salt onto waxed paper; set aside.

2. Melt butter or margarine and chocolate in small saucepan over low heat; add coffee powder and stir to dissolve. Remove pan from heat and let cool.

3. Using wire whisk, beat eggs in large bowl until light and fluffy. Gradually add sugar, stirring with whisk until well blended. Add cooled chocolate mixture and vanilla extract, then flour mixture. Fold in walnuts. Pour into greased 13 x 9 x 2-inch baking pan.

4. Bake for 30 minutes. Cool in pan on wire rack. Cut into 2½-inch squares. *Makes 48.*

MATINEE BRUNCH

CREAMED SEAFOOD
CREPES*

ORANGE AND
ASPARAGUS SALAD

SHERBET DESSERT AND
COOKIES

COFFEE

For eight.

WORK PLAN: A day ahead of time, make Tender Crêpes (page 61).

One and a half hours before serving, line a large shallow platter with leaves from 2 heads of Boston lettuce. Drain three 16-ounce cans asparagus spears and two 11-ounce cans mandarin oranges; arrange in alternate piles on the lettuce. Chill; sprinkle with vinaigrette dressing just before serving. Prepare Creamed Seafood Crêpes (below). Then scoop 2 quarts lemon sherbet into 8 sherbet or champagne glasses; sprinkle with ½ cup chopped nuts and ¼ cup grated chocolate and freeze until serving time. Serve with rolled cookies.

Brew coffee to serve with meal.

CREAMED SEAFOOD CREPES

Tender Crêpes (page 61)
1 cup chopped mushrooms
¼ cup finely chopped onion
¼ cup chopped green onion
1 cup dry white wine
¼ cup butter or margarine
1 cup heavy cream
salt and white pepper to
    taste
2 tablespoons cornstarch
¼ cup cold water
1 cup grated sharp Cheddar
    cheese
one 6-ounce can crabmeat,
    drained and cartilage
    removed
one 4½-ounce can shrimp,
    drained and rinsed in cold
    water

1. Make Tender Crêpes and store as directed in note.

2. Simmer mushrooms, onion and green onion in wine in medium skillet until liquid is reduced by one half. Stir in butter or margarine, cream, salt and pepper.

3. In small bowl, stir cornstarch into cold water until smooth. Add to mushroom-wine mixture. Cook over medium heat, stirring constantly, until mixture thickens and bubbles, about 3 minutes. Stir in cheese, crabmeat and shrimp and heat just until cheese melts.

4. Fill each crêpe with 2 tablespoons seafood mixture. Roll up and serve.

Note: To keep Creamed Seafood Crêpes warm, place in greased baking dish in 200° F oven. If you wish, sprinkle more grated cheese on top and place under broiler until melted.

Tender Crêpes

4 whole eggs
1 egg yolk
2 cups milk
½ cup butter or margarine,
   melted
2 cups flour
1 teaspoon salt
butter

1. Using electric mixer at medium speed, beat whole eggs, egg yolk, milk and melted butter or margarine in medium bowl until blended. Add flour and salt; beat until smooth. Refrigerate for 1 hour.

2. Heat 7-inch crêpe pan or small skillet over medium heat; brush lightly with butter and heat 30 seconds longer. Pour ¼ cup batter into pan; tilt pan to coat evenly. Cook for about 1 minute or until lightly browned on bottom; turn and cook 1 minute longer. Repeat to use remaining batter. Cool crêpes slightly before filling. *Makes about 20.*

Note: If desired, make crêpes a day ahead of time. Cool by stacking between sheets of waxed paper. Overwrap with plastic wrap or foil and store in refrigerator. (Or freeze if storing more than 1 day.) To reheat, unwrap and place in single overlapping layer on baking sheet; cover with damp towel and heat at 300° F for 5 minutes.

BUFFET INTERNATIONALE

CRISP CHICKEN KIEV*

CORN PONES*

BROCCOLI WITH
HOLLANDAISE SAUCE

CUSTARD AMORE*

BAKED FRUIT*

NUT CHOCOLATE
GRAHAMS*

For twelve.

WORK PLAN: About 2½ hours before serving, prepare Custard Amore (page 63). Prepare Crisp Chicken Kiev through Step 4 (see recipe page 62); 30 minutes before serving, cook chicken as directed and keep warm. (Or make chicken ahead, freeze and reheat as directed.)

About an hour ahead of time, make Corn Pones (page 62). Prepare Baked Fruit and Nut Chocolate Grahams (page 63); bake together. Next, wash and trim 4 pounds fresh broccoli; cut into spears and cook in 1 cup boiling salted water until just tender, about 15 to 20 minutes. To make hollandaise sauce, combine 6 egg yolks, ¼ cup lemon juice, 1 teaspoon salt and 6 drops hot pepper sauce in blender at low speed. With blender at high speed, slowly pour in 1 cup butter or margarine, melted. Place blender container in saucepan of hot (not boiling) water to heat sauce, stirring from time to time.

CRISP CHICKEN KIEV

1 cup butter or margarine, softened
2 tablespoons chopped parsley
1 clove garlic, crushed
1 teaspoon crumbled tarragon
¾ teaspoon salt
½ teaspoon crumbled marjoram
½ teaspoon crumbled basil
⅛ teaspoon pepper
6 large whole chicken breasts
¾ cup flour
3 large eggs
2 cups packaged cornflake crumbs
½ cup sesame seeds
oil for deep frying

1. In medium bowl, mix butter or margarine, parsley, garlic, tarragon, salt, marjoram, basil and pepper until thoroughly blended. Shape into 6-inch square; freeze on heavy-duty aluminum foil until firm, about 40 minutes.

2. Pull skin from chicken breasts; halve breasts and cut meat in one piece from bones. Place each half boned side up between two pieces of waxed paper; using wooden mallet or rolling pin, pound to ¼-inch thickness (be careful not to pound holes in meat).

3. Cut frozen butter or margarine into 12 pats. Place a pat in center of each chicken piece. Bring long sides of chicken over filling. Fold ends of chicken over so that no butter shows. Fasten with wooden toothpicks.

4. Roll each chicken piece in flour. Beat eggs in small bowl; combine cornflakes and sesame seeds in another small bowl. Dip each chicken piece into eggs, then in crumbs, coating evenly. Refrigerate, covered, for about 1 hour.

5. Heat 3 inches oil in deep fat fryer to 390° F. Add chicken pieces three at a time and fry, turning frequently, until brown and tender, no more than 5 minutes. Remove carefully with tongs. Drain on paper towel-lined platter; keep warm in 200° F oven.

Note: After Crisp Chicken Kiev is fried and cooled, it can be wrapped in foil and frozen. To serve, unwrap and place immediately in 13 x 9 x 2-inch baking pan; heat in 350° F for 35 minutes.

CORN PONES

6 cups cornmeal
4½ teaspoons salt
boiling water
bacon drippings or melted butter or margarine, cooled

1. Preheat oven to 400° F.

2. In large bowl, combine cornmeal and salt; blend well. Slowly add enough boiling water to make soft, moist dough that holds its shape.

3. Dip hands in bacon drippings or melted butter or margarine. Form dough into 2½ x 1½ x ½-inch ovals. Place on baking sheet or in jelly-roll pan. Bake for 40 to 45 minutes, until golden and crispy but still tender inside.

CUSTARD AMORE

4 cups milk
6 eggs
1 cup sugar
¼ teaspoon salt
½ cup anise liqueur
1 teaspoon vanilla extract
nutmeg

1. Scald milk in large saucepan over low heat.

2. Using electric mixer at medium speed, beat eggs in medium bowl. Slowly add sugar and salt; blend well.

3. Pour ½ cup of the scalded milk into egg mixture, then return to saucepan. Cook over very low heat, stirring constantly until thick enough to coat back of metal spoon. (Do not rush this step or custard will curdle.) Pour into medium bowl; stir to cool, then cover with plastic wrap. Refrigerate custard until chilled, 1 to 1½ hours.

4. Using wire whisk, gently stir anise liqueur and vanilla extract into custard. Pour into 8 punch cups; sprinkle with nutmeg. Refrigerate until serving time.

BAKED FRUIT

one 16-ounce can peaches
one 16-ounce can pears
one 16-ounce can apricots
¼ cup brown sugar, firmly
** packed**
½ teaspoon cinnamon
¼ teaspoon nutmeg
⅛ teaspoon salt
2 tablespoons butter or
** margarine**

1. Drain peaches, pears and apricots, reserving ¾ cup juice. Arrange fruit in greased, large shallow casserole.

2. Combine reserved fruit juice, brown sugar, cinnamon, nutmeg and salt. Pour over fruit. Dot with tiny pieces of butter or margarine. Bake at 350° F for 30 minutes, until hot and bubbly.

NUT CHOCOLATE GRAHAMS

4 ounces graham crackers,
** crumbled**
1 cup broken pecans
½ cup margarine
3 tablespoons butter
one 1-ounce square
** unsweetened chocolate**
⅔ cup sugar

1. Line 15 x 10 x 1-inch jelly-roll pan with crumbled graham crackers. Sprinkle broken pecans over crackers.

2. Melt margarine, butter and chocolate in small saucepan over low heat; add sugar and stir until dissolved. Pour over crackers and nuts.

3. Bake at 350° F for 8 minutes. Invert immediately onto sheet of heavy-duty aluminum foil; cool completely. Slice with long sharp knife.

OLD SOUTH BUFFET

WHOLE PORK SHOULDER
WITH CORNMEAL
CREPES*

SAVORY BAKED APPLES*

COLESLAW

PEAS AND CARROTS

SOUTHERN LEMON PIE*

For twelve.

WORK PLAN: About 3 hours before serving, prepare Whole Pork Shoulder (below). Then make Southern Lemon Pie (page 65). For coleslaw, combine 6 cups finely shredded cabbage, 3 cups each shredded carrots and thinly sliced apples, 2 cups sour cream, 1 tablespoon sugar, 2 teaspoons salt and ½ teaspoon pepper; chill until serving time. Prepare Cornmeal Crêpes (below); keep warm as directed until serving time. Prepare Savory Baked Apples (page 65). Finally, cook two 32-ounce polybags frozen peas and carrots according to label directions.

WHOLE PORK SHOULDER WITH CORNMEAL CRÊPES

**5-pound bone-in pork
   shoulder (butt portion)**
**1 tablespoon mixed pickling
   spices**
1 onion, sliced
Cornmeal Crêpes (below)
**one 16-ounce bottle hickory-
   flavored barbecue sauce**

1. Place pork, pickling spices and onion in large saucepan. Add water to cover.

2. Bring to just below boiling point; cover pan and reduce heat to low. Simmer for 2½ hours (or 30 minutes per pound), until pork is fork-tender. Drain from liquid. Let cool slightly, then slice thinly.

3. Meanwhile, make Cornmeal Crêpes; keep warm. Heat barbecue sauce. Fill crêpes with sliced pork and hot barbecue sauce. Roll and serve immediately.

Cornmeal Crêpes

**1⅓ cups yellow stone-
   ground cornmeal**
2 cups flour
2 teaspoons salt
2 teaspoons baking soda
2½ cups water
1⅓ cups evaporated milk
3 eggs
butter or vegetable oil

1. In large bowl, combine cornmeal, flour, salt and baking soda. Add water, evaporated milk and eggs; beat with wire whisk until smooth. Refrigerate for at least 1 hour.

2. Heat 7-inch crêpe pan or small skillet over medium heat; brush lightly with butter or oil. Heat 30 seconds longer. Pour scant ¼ cup batter into pan; tilt pan to coat evenly. Cook for about 1 minute, until lightly browned on bottom; turn and cook 1 minute longer. Remove and roll up. Repeat with remaining batter. To keep crêpes warm, place on heated platter. *Makes 40.*

Note: These crêpes can be made ahead. Cool by stacking them between sheets of waxed paper. Overwrap with plastic wrap or foil, and freeze. Thaw and unwrap. To reheat, place in single overlapping layer on baking sheet; cover with damp towel and heat in 300° F oven for 5 minutes.

SAVORY BAKED APPLES

1 pound sliced bacon
12 medium apples
1 cup golden raisins
2 teaspoons salt
2 teaspoons sage
2 teaspoons onion powder
1 cup water

1. Fry bacon in large skillet over medium heat until crisp. Drain on paper towels and crumble; reserve bacon fat.

2. Core apples and prick all over with fork; place in large shallow baking dish.

3. Combine bacon, raisins, salt, sage and onion powder; fill centers of apples with mixture. Pour reserved bacon fat over apples; add water to baking dish. Bake at 350° F for 20 to 30 minutes, until tender.

SOUTHERN LEMON PIE

3 cups sugar
2 tablespoons flour
2 tablespoons cornmeal
½ teaspoon salt
8 eggs
3 tablespoons grated lemon
 rind
⅔ cup fresh lemon juice
two 9-inch unbaked pie
 shells

1. Preheat oven to 325° F.

2. In large bowl, combine sugar, flour, cornmeal and salt; toss lightly with fork until blended. Add eggs, lemon rind and lemon juice. Using electric mixer at medium speed, beat until smooth.

3. Divide mixture between pie shells. Bake for 40 minutes or until firm and golden brown. *Makes two 9-inch pies.*

Custard pies like the Southern Lemon Pie, above, are easy-on-the-cook desserts that are ideal for topping off a traditional pork or ham meal. The basic egg filling can be flavored in a variety of ways—with different extracts like vanilla and almond, with brown sugar, chopped nuts, raisins, dates or coconut—for a myriad of delicious desserts.

PARK AVENUE BUFFET

HAM AND MUSHROOM
CANAPES*

BEEF BURGUNDY*

GRAPEFRUIT-AVOCADO-
RED ONION SALAD*

GREEN BEANS AND
WATER CHESTNUTS

COCONUT CAKE*

For twelve.

WORK PLAN: A day ahead of time, do Steps 1 through 4 of Coconut Cake (see recipe page 68); store cake layers and grated coconut in airtight containers. Make Ham and Mushroom Canapes (below); the next day, reheat with Beef Burgundy for 15 minutes.

Four and a half hours before serving, prepare Beef Burgundy (page 67) and finish Coconut Cake. Next, make Grapefruit-Avocado-Red Onion Salad (page 67); toss with dressing just before serving.

About 30 minutes before serving time, wash and trim 4 pounds fresh green beans; cook in boiling salted water to cover until just tender, about 8 minutes (or cook two 32-ounce polybags frozen whole green beans according to label directions); drain. Toss with two 7-ounce cans water chestnuts, drained and sliced, and ½ cup butter or margarine; reheat.

HAM AND MUSHROOM CANAPES

1 cup butter or margarine
one 8-ounce package cream
  cheese
2¼ cups flour
½ teaspoon salt
¼ teaspoon cayenne pepper
¼ teaspoon paprika
2 tablespoons butter or
  margarine
1 cup finely chopped
  mushrooms
⅓ cup finely chopped onion
2 tablespoons flour
one 4½-ounce can deviled
  ham
1 tablespoon chopped
  parsley
1 teaspoon Dijon-style
  mustard
1 egg, slightly beaten

1. Cream 1 cup butter or margarine and the cream cheese in medium bowl until light and fluffy. Add 2¼ cups flour, the salt, cayenne and paprika. Mix just until dough leaves side of bowl and forms a ball. Wrap dough in plastic wrap and refrigerate for 1 hour.

2. Meanwhile, melt 2 tablespoons butter or margarine in small saucepan over medium heat; add mushrooms and onion and sauté until soft, about 3 to 4 minutes. Sprinkle in 2 tablespoons flour and stir until blended. Cook for 2 minutes; remove pan from heat. Stir in deviled ham, parsley and mustard until well blended; let cool.

3. Preheat oven to 400° F.

4. Roll dough out to ⅛-inch thickness on lightly floured board. Cut into 2½-inch rounds. Spoon ½ teaspoon filling on each round. Dampen edge of each round with water; fold rounds in half, then crimp edges with fork.

5. Place on greased sheets. Brush with slightly beaten egg. Bake for 10 minutes or until pastry is golden brown. Serve warm or cool.

Note: If desired, cover cooled canapes and refrigerate overnight; uncover and reheat at 275° F for 15 minutes. Canapes can also be frozen unbaked. Brush with egg, then bake at 350° F for 15 to 20 minutes, until golden.

BEEF BURGUNDY

4-pound round steak,
  2 inches thick
1 cup red Burgundy wine
two 10¾-ounce cans
  condensed cream of
  celery soup
one 10¾-ounce can
  condensed cream of
  mushroom soup
one .75-ounce package
  onion soup mix
4 cups thinly sliced
  mushrooms
hot cooked rice or noodles

1. Cut beef into 1-inch cubes; marinate in wine for 30 minutes at room temperature.

2. Preheat oven to 275° F.

3. In 3- to 4-quart casserole, combine beef and wine, condensed celery soup and mushroom soup, onion soup mix and mushrooms. Cover and bake for 4 hours, until meat is very tender. Serve with rice or noodles.

GRAPEFRUIT-AVOCADO-RED ONION SALAD

6 grapefruit
4 ripe avocados, halved and
  peeled
1 large red onion

DRESSING
¼ cup wine vinegar
¼ cup peanut oil
1 tablespoon water
1 tablespoon sugar
2 teaspoons prepared
  horseradish
1 teaspoon salt
¼ teaspoon pepper

2 tablespoons toasted
  sesame seeds

1. Peel and section grapefruit, removing all white membrane. Slice avocados into thin bite-size pieces. Slice red onion into thin whole slices; separate into circles. Arrange grapefruit, avocados and onion in large salad bowl for easy tossing; cover and chill until ready to serve.

2. To make dressing, combine vinegar, oil, water, sugar, horseradish, salt and pepper in screw-top jar; shake until well blended. Just before serving, shake dressing again and pour over salad; top with toasted sesame seeds.

COCONUT CAKE

**one 18.5-ounce package
  yellow cake mix**
1 fresh coconut
1½ cups sugar
½ cup water
⅛ teaspoon salt
2 egg whites
½ teaspoon almond extract
½ teaspoon vanilla extract

1. Preheat oven to 350° F.

2. Prepare cake mix and bake cake in two 9-inch layer pans according to label directions. Cool and remove from pans as directed.

3. Meanwhile, puncture the 3 indentations at the end of the coconut with long clean nail. Drain off milk and reserve. Place coconut in shallow baking dish and bake for 15 minutes or until shell cracks. Use hammer to complete cracking, then remove meat in large chunks. Using sharp knife, cut skin from meat; grate meat with vegetable grater or food processor; set aside.

4. Pour ⅓ cup reserved coconut milk over each cooled cake layer.

5. Heat sugar, water and salt in small saucepan over low heat until sugar dissolves. Raise heat to high and cook, without stirring, to hard ball stage (260° F on candy thermometer).

6. Using electric mixer at high speed, beat egg whites in medium bowl until stiff. Gradually pour syrup into egg whites, beating constantly. Add almond and vanilla extracts. Continue beating until mixture forms peaks and reaches spreading consistency.

7. Place 1 cake layer on serving platter; spread frosting on top. Sprinkle with grated coconut. Top with second cake layer. Frost top and sides of cake, then sprinkle with coconut. *Makes one 9-inch layer cake.*

Packaged coconut can't come close to the taste of fresh coconut. You'll find the real thing in most fruit and vegetable markets, particularly in late fall and early winter. It takes some time and trouble to deal with cracking the shell, draining the milk and grating the meat, but the results are spectacular. Use fresh coconut for desserts like this Coconut Cake and in cream pies; try it the next time you make an Indian or Polynesian main course to bring a touch of exotic authenticity to your dining table.

COLD WEATHER BUFFET

EGGNOG *

GLAZED HAM *

PEAS AND ONIONS IN CHEESE CUPS *

CORN PUDDING *

SPICY CANDIED PECANS *

GRANDMOTHER'S PLUM CAKE *

LEMON ICE BOX CAKE *

FROZEN ORANGES *

For twelve.

WORK PLAN: A day before serving, begin soaking Glazed Ham (page 70). Then make Spicy Candied Pecans, Grandmother's Plum Cake, Lemon Ice Box Cake and Frozen Oranges (pages 71–72).

Five hours before serving time, complete preparations for Glazed Ham.

One and a half hours before serving, prepare Eggnog (below), then Peas and Onions in Cheese Cups (page 70).

Forty-five minutes before serving time, make Corn Pudding (page 71).

EGGNOG

12 eggs, separated
1¼ cups sugar
4 cups heavy cream
1½ cups rum, chilled
1½ cups blended whiskey, chilled
nutmeg

1. Using electric mixer at high speed, beat egg yolks in large bowl; gradually add 1 cup of the sugar. Stir in cream, chilled rum and whiskey.

2. Using electric mixer at high speed, beat egg whites and remaining ¼ cup sugar in another large bowl until soft peaks form.

3. Fold egg whites into egg yolk mixture. Pour into punch bowl; sprinkle with nutmeg. *Makes 24 servings.*

Note: To make Eggnog ahead of time, prepare egg yolk mixture containing cream and alcohol; chill. Just before serving, beat egg whites and sugar and fold into egg yolk mixture.

GLAZED HAM

14-pound Smithfield ham
whole cloves
brown sugar

1. Cut off butt ends of ham. In large, deep kettle or roasting pan, soak ham in water to cover overnight. The next day, discard water and scrub ham with vegetable brush; rinse well. Return ham to pan; add water to cover.

2. Parboil ham for about 15 minutes; discard water. Add fresh water to cover and parboil again for 15 minutes. Discard water; add fresh water to cover and simmer ham for 4 hours and 40 minutes (or 20 minutes per pound), turning every 2 hours. Let cool in cooking liquid.

3. Preheat oven to 375° F.

4. Remove ham from cooking liquid; trim off and discard all but about ¼ inch of fat. Score fat on ham into 1-inch diamonds; insert cloves where lines cross.

5. Pat top of ham with brown sugar, coating evenly. Bake for 10 to 15 minutes or until sugar melts to form glaze. Let cool completely before slicing very thinly.

PEAS AND ONIONS IN CHEESE CUPS

2 cups flour
1 teaspoon salt
¾ cup vegetable shortening
1 cup grated Cheddar cheese
4 to 6 tablespoons ice water
two 9-ounce packages
** frozen peas and pearl**
** onions**
pimiento slices

1. Preheat oven to 425° F.

2. In medium bowl, mix flour and salt. Using two knives or a pastry blender, cut in shortening until mixture resembles coarse crumbs. Add grated cheese. Sprinkle in ice water, 1 tablespoon at a time; mix in with fork until dough leaves side of bowl and forms a ball.

3. Roll out to ⅛-inch thickness on lightly floured pastry cloth or board. Cut out circles to cover outsides of 12 muffin tins. Bake for 10 to 15 minutes or until golden. Carefully remove from tins and cool on wire racks.

4. Cook peas and onions according to label directions; drain well. Fill cheese cups with hot peas and onions. Top with sliced pimiento. Serve immediately.

CORN PUDDING

2 cups milk
2 tablespoons butter or
  margarine
⅓ cup sugar
¾ teaspoon salt
2½ cups yellow or white
  cornmeal
3 eggs
1 teaspoon mace

1. Preheat oven to 375° F.

2. Scald milk with butter or margarine, sugar and salt in medium saucepan. Let cool slightly.

3. Place half of cornmeal, 1 egg and some of milk mixture in electric blender. Cover and process at high speed for 15 seconds, until smooth. Add remaining cornmeal, 2 eggs, milk mixture and the mace; process until smooth.

4. Pour into greased 2-quart casserole. Place in roasting pan. Place pan in oven, then pour warm water into pan to depth of 1 inch. Bake for 30 minutes or until knife inserted 1 inch from edge comes out clean. Serve immediately.

SPICY CANDIED PECANS

1 cup sugar
½ cup evaporated milk
1 teaspoon cinnamon
½ teaspoon salt
¼ teaspoon nutmeg
2 tablespoons butter or
  margarine
3 cups pecan halves
1 teaspoon vanilla extract

1. In medium-size heavy saucepan, combine sugar, evaporated milk, cinnamon, salt and nutmeg. Boil until mixture reaches soft ball stage (240° F on candy thermometer).

2. Meanwhile, melt butter or margarine in heavy skillet over medium heat; add pecans and sauté for 5 minutes or until lightly toasted. Add to syrup mixture; stir to coat well. Stir in vanilla extract.

3. Pour nuts onto waxed paper. Quickly separate individual halves. Let cool completely. Store in airtight tin.

GRANDMOTHER'S PLUM CAKE

4 cups flour
2 teaspoons baking powder
1 teaspoon salt
1⅓ cups butter or
  margarine, softened
2⅔ cups sugar
4 eggs
1 cup water
1½ teaspoons vanilla extract
three 16-ounce boxes raisins

1. Preheat oven to 300° F. Sift 3¾ cups of the flour, the baking powder and salt onto waxed paper.

2. In large bowl, cream butter or margarine and sugar until light and fluffy. Add eggs one at a time, beating well after each addition. Add sifted dry ingredients alternately with water and vanilla extract. Dust raisins with remaining ¼ cup flour; fold into batter.

3. Spoon into greased 10-inch fluted tube pan or 2 greased 9 x 5 x 3-inch loaf pans. Bake for 1½ hours or until cake springs back when lightly touched and cake tester inserted in center comes out clean. Cool in pan(s) on wire rack for 25 minutes. Loosen cake around edges and tube with sharp knife; invert onto rack to cool completely. *Makes one 10-inch tube cake or 2 loaf cakes.*

LEMON ICE BOX CAKE

¼ cup granulated sugar
1 tablespoon cornstarch
3 eggs, separated
¼ cup milk
1 tablespoon lemon juice
1 teaspoon grated lemon
   rind
½ cup butter or margarine
1 cup confectioners' sugar
12 ladyfingers, split
1 cup heavy cream
¼ cup chopped walnuts

1. In top of double boiler, blend granulated sugar and cornstarch.

2. Using electric mixer at high speed, beat egg yolks and milk in small bowl; add to sugar mixture. Cook over boiling water, stirring constantly, until mixture thickens. Remove from hot water. Add lemon juice and lemon rind; let cool.

3. In small bowl, cream butter or margarine and confectioners' sugar; stir into cooled lemon mixture. Using electric mixer at high speed, beat egg whites in another small bowl until stiff; fold into lemon mixture.

4. Line bottom of 9 x 5 x 3-inch loaf pan with waxed paper. Place split ladyfingers in bottom and along sides of pan. Pour in lemon mixture. Refrigerate for at least 12 hours or overnight.

5. At serving time, beat cream until stiff. Run thin-bladed knife around edges of pan; invert onto long serving plate. Cover with beaten cream and sprinkle with walnuts. *Makes 1 loaf cake.*

FROZEN ORANGES

9 egg yolks
1 cup sugar
½ cup orange liqueur
4 cups heavy cream
12 oranges
grated orange rind

1. Using electric mixer at medium speed, beat egg yolks and sugar in large bowl. Continue beating while slowly trickling in liqueur.

2. Beat 3 cups of the cream in another bowl until stiff. Fold into egg mixture.

3. Cut tops off oranges. Using teaspoon, remove pulp and reserve for another use. Fill orange shells with egg-cream mixture and freeze for at least 4 hours or overnight.

4. At serving time, stiffly beat remaining 1 cup cream; spoon on top of orange shells. Garnish with orange rind.

Note: If desired, egg-cream mixture may be turned into a 1½-quart soufflé dish with a collar. Freeze and top with beaten cream and orange rind as directed above.

HEARTY HOLIDAY BUFFET

BEEF WELLINGTON*

POTATO SOUFFLE*

VEGETABLE BOUQUET WITH CHEESE SAUCE*

BAKED PEARS*

CHOCOLATE WHIPPED CREAM CAKE*

For eight.

BEEF WELLINGTON

WORK PLAN: At least 3 hours before serving, begin preparing Beef Wellington (below); bake after Potato Soufflé comes out of oven. Prepare Chocolate Whipped Cream Cake (page 75).

Forty-five minutes before serving time, make Potato Soufflé (page 74) and Baked Pears (page 75); bake these two dishes together. Prepare Vegetable Bouquet with Cheese Sauce (page 74). Return Potato Soufflé to oven during last 5 minutes of Beef Wellington's cooking time.

4-pound beef fillet
2 tablespoons butter or margarine, softened
salt and pepper
½ cup chopped celery
½ cup chopped onion
½ cup chopped carrot
2 tablespoons dried marjoram
2 tablespoons chopped parsley
one 10-ounce package frozen patty shells
Pâté for Beef Wellington (page 74)
1 egg
1 tablespoon water
watercress sprigs, cherry tomatoes

1. Preheat oven to 450° F.

2. Coat fillet with softened butter or margarine and season with salt and pepper. Sprinkle celery, onion, carrot, marjoram and parsley in bottom of large roasting pan. Place fillet over vegetables. Roast for 30 minutes. Remove fillet from pan and cool completely; reserve vegetables for pâté. Reduce oven temperature to 425° F.

3. Remove patty shells from freezer and separate. Let stand at room temperature for 20 minutes. Arrange patty shells in slightly overlapping double row on lightly floured board; roll out to ¼-inch thickness.

4. Meanwhile, make Pâté for Beef Wellington. Completely cover cooled fillet with pâté. Wrap in pastry; reserve trimmings. Moisten edges with water and press to seal. Place seam side down on large baking sheet.

5. Beat together egg and water; brush pastry well with part of mixture. Cut reserved pastry trimmings into patterns; arrange on top. Brush with remaining egg mixture. Prick pastry several times. Bake for 20 minutes or until pastry is golden. Slide onto heated serving platter and garnish with watercress and cherry tomatoes. Slice thinly.

Pâté for Beef Wellington

½ cup butter or margarine
1 pound chicken livers, washed and trimmed of fat
½ cup chopped onion
¾ cup chopped mushrooms
1 tablespoon brandy
½ teaspoon freshly ground black pepper
½ teaspoon mace
¼ teaspoon thyme
¼ teaspoon ginger
⅛ teaspoon cayenne pepper
⅛ teaspoon white pepper
1 cup reserved vegetables from roast

1. Melt ¼ cup of the butter or margarine in medium skillet over medium heat; add chicken livers and onion and sauté until livers are brown on the outside but still pink inside. Remove to electric blender container with slotted spoon.

2. Add mushrooms to drippings in skillet; sauté until soft, about 3 to 4 minutes. Add mushrooms with drippings to livers and onion in blender.

3. Add remaining ¼ cup butter or margarine, the brandy, black pepper, mace, thyme, ginger, cayenne and white pepper to blender. Cover and process at high speed for 30 seconds or until smooth and of spreading consistency. If necessary, add a few more drops of brandy and process for several seconds. *Makes enough to cover one 4-pound beef fillet.*

POTATO SOUFFLE

2 cups instant mashed potato flakes
1 cup unflavored yogurt
one 8-ounce package cream cheese
¾ cup chopped green onions
2 eggs, well beaten
½ cup grated Parmesan cheese

1. Preheat oven to 350° F.

2. Prepare instant mashed potatoes in large saucepan according to label directions. Blend in yogurt, cream cheese and green onions. Fold in beaten eggs. Turn into greased 2-quart casserole. Sprinkle with grated Parmesan cheese.

3. Bake for 45 minutes or until puffy and golden.

Note: This recipe can easily be doubled; bake soufflé in two 2-quart casseroles.

VEGETABLE BOUQUET WITH CHEESE SAUCE

1 head cauliflower (about 1 pound)
1 bunch broccoli (about 1 pound)
½ pound carrots
1 tablespoon salt
1 teaspoon sugar
one 6-ounce can button mushrooms, drained
Cheese Sauce (page 75)

1. Soak cauliflower and broccoli in cold salted water to cover. Trim broccoli, throwing away leaves and tough part of stems; cut into spears. Remove center core from cauliflower. Peel carrots and cut into 1-inch diagonal pieces.

2. Place steamer or metal collander in large kettle; add water up to bottom of steamer along with salt and sugar. Place carrots in bottom of steamer, then cauliflower in center and broccoli on sides. Top with drained mushrooms. Steam for 20 minutes or until crisp-tender.

3. Meanwhile, make Cheese Sauce; serve over hot Vegetable Bouquet.

Cheese Sauce

**2 tablespoons butter or
  margarine**
2 teaspoons flour
1 cup milk
**1 cup grated longhorn
  cheese**
½ teaspoon salt
½ teaspoon cayenne pepper
½ teaspoon paprika
¼ teaspoon chili powder
1 egg, well beaten

1. Melt butter or margarine in small saucepan over low heat; blend in flour. Add milk gradually, stirring constantly. Cook, stirring frequently, until sauce begins to thicken. Blend in grated cheese, salt, cayenne, paprika and chili powder.

2. Add a small amount of cheese mixture to well-beaten egg. Stir egg mixture into remaining cheese sauce until well blended. To insure smoothness, place sauce in blender and process at high speed for 30 seconds. *Makes about 2 cups.*

BAKED PEARS

**two 29-ounce cans pear
  halves, drained**
grenadine syrup
brown or granulated sugar
butter or margarine
salt
freshly grated nutmeg

1. Place drained pears in large casserole. Place ½ teaspoon grenadine syrup and ½ teaspoon sugar in hollow of each pear half. Dot with thin sliver of butter or margarine and a pinch of salt. Sprinkle grated nutmeg over top.

2. Bake pears at 350° F for 20 minutes or until hot and bubbly. Serve warm or cool.

CHOCOLATE WHIPPED CREAM CAKE

**one 18.5-ounce package
  devil's food cake mix**
1 pint heavy cream
¼ cup confectioners' sugar
1 teaspoon vanilla extract
½ teaspoon almond extract
**one 1-ounce square
  unsweetened chocolate**

1. Prepare cake mix and bake layer cake according to label directions. Cool and remove from pans as directed.

2. Using electric mixer at high speed, beat cream in small bowl until stiff. Beat in confectioners' sugar and vanilla and almond extracts.

3. Fill and frost cake with beaten cream mixture. Grate chocolate over top. Chill, uncovered, in refrigerator until serving time. *Makes one 2-layer cake.*

EAST/WEST BUFFET

CHICKEN TERIYAKI*

FETA-SPINACH
TURNOVERS*

MARINATED CARROTS

BAKED STUFFED
TOMATOES

DEVILISHLY DIVINE
CAKE*

For twelve.

WORK PLAN: About 5 hours before serving, start Chicken Teriyaki (below); about 15 minutes before serving, drain chicken from marinade and broil as directed. Prepare Feta-Spinach Turnovers (page 77), then reduce oven temperature and bake Devilishly Divine Cake (page 78). Next, peel 4 pounds carrots; cut into 2-inch julienne strips. Cook in boiling salted water to cover just until tender; drain well. While hot, toss with 1½ cups oil and vinegar dressing and ¾ cup chopped parsley; chill until serving time. Prepare baked stuffed tomatoes: Cut off tops of 12 large tomatoes; using teaspoon, scoop out pulp and seeds. Place tomatoes in large shallow baking dish; fill centers with one 16-ounce package herb stuffing mix prepared according to label directions. Add 1 cup water to baking dish and bake at 375° F for 20 to 25 minutes, until tomatoes are tender and stuffing is very hot. *Pictured on page 102.*

CHICKEN TERIYAKI

8 whole chicken breasts
1 cup soy sauce
½ cup dry sherry
2 tablespoons sugar
1 tablespoon finely grated ginger root, or 1½ teaspoons powdered ginger
1 clove garlic, crushed

1. Bone chicken and cut in half, keeping skin on. Place chicken in shallow dish.

2. In small bowl, combine soy sauce, dry sherry, sugar, ginger and garlic; pour over chicken. Marinate in refrigerator for at least 4 hours, stirring every hour.

3. Remove chicken from marinade, reserving marinade. Barbecue or oven-broil chicken 5 inches from heat, frequently turning and brushing with marinade, for 8 to 10 minutes or until skin is crisp and meat is tender. Serve with remaining marinade.

Note: If you wish to remove skin from chicken, add ¼ cup oil to marinade.

FETA-SPINACH TURNOVERS (FETISHES)

1 pound feta cheese
two 10-ounce packages
frozen chopped spinach,
thawed
2 cups butter or margarine
1 cup finely chopped onion
1 cup thinly sliced
mushrooms
1 pound boiled ham, finely
chopped
2 eggs, beaten
salt and pepper to taste
one 16-ounce package filo
leaves

1. Preheat oven to 400° F.

2. Dice feta cheese; set aside. Press spinach in strainer or colander to remove all moisture; spinach should be as dry as possible. Set aside.

3. Melt 2 tablespoons of the butter or margarine in large skillet over medium heat; add onion and mushrooms and sauté for 4 minutes, until tender. Stir in ham; sauté 3 to 4 minutes longer. Turn into large bowl; let cool to room temperature. Stir in beaten eggs, feta, spinach, salt and pepper; mix well.

4. Melt remaining butter or margarine in small saucepan. To assemble turnovers, use 1 filo leaf at a time, keeping others covered with a piece of waxed paper and a dampened paper towel to prevent drying out. Brush 1 filo leaf with melted butter or margarine. Place scant ¼ cup spinach-cheese filling on filo leaf on center of short edge nearest you. Fold both long sides to meet over filling, forming a long rectangle; butter surface of folded sides. Fold one corner of pastry nearest you over filling, forming a triangle at bottom of rectangle. Continue folding in triangles, buttering surface of filo, until other end of rectangle is reached. Butter end and top of triangular package.

5. Repeat buttering, filling and folding filo leaves to make 24 turnovers. Arrange on baking sheets or in jelly-roll pans. Bake for 12 to 15 minutes or until golden brown and very flaky. *Makes 24.*

Note: These pastries freeze well baked or unbaked. If freezing unbaked, allow an additional 5 to 6 minutes baking time for the frozen pastries.

Filo (also spelled phyllo) is tricky to work with, but nothing can duplicate the wonderfully light, flaky pastry that results when the leaves are individually buttered and layered. You'll be wise to enlist a cook's assistant when a dish involving filo is on your party menu—you'll be able to work twice as fast, and the leaves won't be likely to dry out. Look for 16-ounce packages of filo leaves at food import shops and Middle Eastern grocery stores.

DEVILISHLY DIVINE CAKE

1 cup butter or margarine
1 cup water
⅓ cup unsweetened cocoa
  powder
2 cups flour
2 cups sugar
1 teaspoon salt
1 teaspoon baking soda
2 eggs
½ cup unflavored yogurt
Chocolate-Nut Frosting
  (below)

1. Preheat oven to 350° F.

2. In small saucepan, combine butter or margarine, water and cocoa; bring to boiling point. Remove pan from heat and let cool.

3. Sift flour, sugar, salt and baking soda onto waxed paper.

4. Using electric mixer at medium speed, beat eggs in large bowl. With mixer at low speed, stir in yogurt, then stir in dry ingredients and cooled chocolate mixture. Pour batter into greased 9-inch tube pan.

5. Bake for 25 to 30 minutes or until cake springs back when lightly touched and toothpick inserted in center comes out clean. Cool in pan on wire rack for 10 minutes. Loosen cake around tube and edge with knife; invert onto wire rack and cool completely. Ice with Chocolate-Nut Frosting. *Makes one 9-inch tube cake.*

Chocolate-Nut Frosting

½ cup butter or margarine
⅓ cup milk
⅓ cup unsweetened cocoa
  powder
one 16-ounce box
  confectioners' sugar
1 teaspoon vanilla extract
½ teaspoon salt
1 cup chopped pecans

1. Heat butter or margarine, milk and cocoa in medium saucepan over low heat just until butter or margarine melts. Remove pan from heat.

2. Using electric mixer at high speed, beat in confectioners' sugar, vanilla extract and salt. Fold in pecans. Spread while warm onto cooled cake. *Makes enough for one 9-inch tube cake.*

Holidays and Birthdays

Holidays and special family events are joyous occasions that deserve full-fledged celebrations. Take the fuss out of these fancy meals with the menus in this chapter. With the work plans spelling out every step in the preparation, all dishes will be ready when the dinner bell rings.

This chapter is chock-full of delicious new variations on traditional themes. The usual Independence Day fried-chicken-and-potato-salad spread gets a new All-American look with a Fourth of July Feast that features Salmon in Puff Pastry, grilled sirloin steak and chicken breasts, and Firecracker Sundaes. Thrill the Thanksgiving crowd by dressing the turkey with an unusually flavored Apple-Sausage Stuffing and baking a Toasty Chestnut Stuffing to serve alongside; break with tradition and offer homemade raw cranberry relish with baked squash. Show off your culinary skills at Christmas by following up your Holiday Rib Roast with a buffet of desserts like Aunt Bess's Lemon Chess Pie and Plum Duff.

These big-event parties don't stop with traditional holidays. In June honor a new graduate at a party where you serve Gretchen's Taco Salad and Diploma Cookies. Celebrate spring early—have some friends in on March 17 for a bit of blarney and a Saint Patrick's Day Hearty Stew.

Don't forget that each member of your family has his or her own special day. Whether you want to host an afternoon of games and lunch for the grade-school set, surprise your spouse or plan a celebration for a good friend, you'll find ideas here that will make it a birthday to remember.

Is there a "big event" on your calendar? Pick one of the special menus that follow and celebrate in style.

NEW YEAR'S EVE BUFFET DINNER

BELL RINGER SPREAD*

CRACKERS AND
CRISP VEGETABLES

SCALLOPED OYSTERS*

SMITHFIELD HAM

BLACKEYE PEAS*

PINK GRAPEFRUIT SALAD
WREATH*

BISCUITS AND BUTTER
ROLLS

RICH MOIST DRIED-FRUIT
CAKE*

PINWHEEL CHARLOTTE
RUSSE*

CRUNCHI-FRUITTI ICE
CREAM*

CHAMPAGNE

PLENTY OF HOT COFFEE

For ten to twelve.

WORK PLAN: About 3 or 4 weeks ahead of time, make Rich Moist Dried-Fruit Cake (page 82). A day or two ahead of time, make Crunchi-Fruitti Ice Cream (page 83). Carefully follow storage and additional serving instructions. A day or two ahead, soak and boil one 12- to 18-pound Smithfield ham according to label directions. Cool completely and cover in plastic wrap; refrigerate until serving time.

Six hours ahead of time, prepare Pinwheel Charlotte Russe (page 83). A few hours before serving, make Bell Ringer Spread (page 81) to serve with crackers and crisp vegetables. Prepare Blackeye Peas (page 81); reheat just before serving. Next, make Pink Grapefruit Salad Wreath (page 82), and prepare dressing just before serving. For biscuits, prepare 4 cups packaged biscuit mix according to label directions; knead dough for 5 minutes before rolling to ½-inch thickness and cutting into 1½-inch rounds. Bake according to label directions for 5 to 7 minutes, until pale golden and crisp. For rolls, prepare four 8-ounce packages refrigerator crescent rolls according to label directions, spreading each with a little softened butter or margarine before rolling; bake according to label directions. Make Scalloped Oysters (page 81). Reheat biscuits and rolls in aluminum foil while oysters bake.

Serve champagne at party and brew plenty of after-dinner coffee.

BELL RINGER SPREAD

one 8-ounce package cream
   cheese, softened
½ cup shredded sharp
   Cheddar cheese
3 tablespoons chopped
   pimiento, or 2 ounces red
   caviar
2 to 3 drops hot pepper
   sauce

1. In medium bowl, thoroughly mix cream cheese, shredded Cheddar cheese, 2 tablespoons of the pimiento or about two-thirds of the red caviar, and the hot pepper sauce.

2. Mound the cheese mixture on a serving plate, then use frosting spatula to shape mixture into a bell. If mixture seems too stiff to shape easily, blend in a little milk or cream. Outline the bell shape with remaining pimiento or caviar. Cover with plastic wrap and refrigerate until serving time.

3. Pass the cheese bell with wheat crackers, melba rounds and crisp sticks or rounds of celery, carrots, cucumber and cauliflower.

SCALLOPED OYSTERS

3 pints fresh oysters
5 cups salted cracker
   crumbs
1 cup butter or margarine,
   melted
1 teaspoon salt
⅛ teaspoon pepper
¾ cup light cream or
   half-and-half
½ teaspoon Worcestershire
   sauce

1. Preheat oven to 350° F.

2. Drain oysters, reserving ¼ cup liquor. Mix cracker crumbs, melted butter or margarine, salt and pepper.

3. Spread oysters in bottom of 3 greased 8-inch pie plates or shallow casseroles or 1 greased 13 x 9 x 2-inch baking dish. Spread 4 cups of the crumb mixture over oysters.

4. Mix cream or half-and-half, reserved oyster liquor and Worcestershire sauce; pour over oysters. Sprinkle with remaining 1 cup crumb mixture. Bake for 30 minutes.

BLACKEYE PEAS

one 16-ounce package dried
   blackeye peas
2 quarts cold water
1 ham bone or large pork
   bone
1 medium onion, sliced
1 small clove garlic, crushed
salt and pepper to taste
4 to 6 drops hot pepper
   sauce

1. Cover peas with cold water, bring to boiling point and simmer for 1 minute; drain. (Or cover peas with water and soak overnight; drain.)

2. Cover drained peas with 2 quarts cold water. Add ham or pork bone, onion and garlic. Bring to boiling point.

3. Reduce heat to medium and simmer for 2 hours. If liquid cooks away too rapidly, add ham broth, if available, water or apple juice. Remove bone, dice meat and return meat to peas.

4. If peas are still very firm, cook 15 minutes longer. Season with salt, pepper and hot pepper sauce.

PINK GRAPEFRUIT SALAD WREATH

**4 large pink grapefruit
watercress or curly endive**

DRESSING
¾ cup vegetable oil
⅓ cup vinegar
**1½ tablespoons sesame
   seeds**
1½ tablespoons sugar
1 tablespoon ketchup
1 teaspoon salt
¼ teaspoon paprika

1. Peel and section grapefruit. Arrange watercress or curly endive on large round serving plate. Place grapefruit segments on greens around edge of plate in spoke fashion. Chill until serving time.

2. Set small bowl in center of plate to hold dressing. To make dressing, combine oil, vinegar, sesame seeds, sugar, ketchup, salt and paprika in screwtop pint jar. Shake vigorously until thoroughly blended. Pour dressing into bowl and serve at once.

RICH MOIST DRIED-FRUIT CAKE

2 cups dark raisins
**2 cups chopped dried pears
   or golden raisins**
2 cups chopped dried apples
**1½ cups coarsely chopped
   candied cherries**
**1½ cups chopped dried
   pineapple**
1 cup chopped dates
**1 cup broken pecans or
   walnuts**
1 cup brandy or apple juice
3 cups butter or margarine
2½ cups sugar
12 eggs
one 12-ounce jar molasses
**1 tablespoon dried or
   freshly grated orange rind**
**1 tablespoon dried or
   freshly grated lemon rind**
1 tablespoon vanilla extract
7 cups flour
2 teaspoons baking soda
2 teaspoons salt
2 tablespoons cinnamon
2 tablespoons nutmeg
1 tablespoon cloves
**brandy- or apple juice-
   soaked cheesecloth**

1. Twenty-four hours before mixing cake, combine dark raisins, pears or golden raisins, apples, cherries, pineapple, dates and nuts. Pour brandy or apple juice over mixture. Stir and toss until liquid is thoroughly mixed in. Tightly cover bowl with plastic wrap. Let stand at room temperature for 24 hours. Toss again before mixing with cake batter.

2. Preheat oven to 300° F. Grease and flour four 9 x 5 x 3-inch loaf pans, or one 9-inch springform pan along with five 6 x 4 x 2½-inch foil loaf pans; line bottoms of pans with waxed paper.

3. In large bowl, cream butter or margarine and sugar. Add eggs one at a time, beating well after each addition. Beat molasses, orange rind, lemon rind and vanilla extract into mixture.

4. Sift flour with baking soda and salt. Sift again with cinnamon, nutmeg and cloves. Add dry ingredients, 2 cups at a time, to creamed mixture, beating until smooth after each addition. Pour batter over prepared fruit. Using wooden spoon, thoroughly blend mixture.

5. Pour into prepared pans. Bake large cakes for 2 hours, smaller cakes 1 to 1½ hours, until cake tester inserted in center comes out clean. Cool in pans on wire racks; wrap individually in brandy- or apple juice-soaked cheesecloth and store in tightly covered containers for 3 to 4 weeks. If desired, soak cheesecloth with brandy or apple juice 2 or 3 times while cakes age. *Makes 4 large loaf cakes.*

Note: Cakes may be left plain or decorated with bits of fruit and nuts. Set and glaze decorations by spooning melted currant jelly over tops of cakes. To make large cake more festive, use a wet knife or frosting spatula to spread ½ pound almond paste on top of cake. Cover the almond paste with glaze made by combining 2 tablespoons brandy with 1¼ cups confectioners' sugar and blending until smooth. Decorate with candied cherries, pieces of dried fruit and nuts.

PINWHEEL CHARLOTTE RUSSE

2 envelopes unflavored
   gelatin
½ cup cold water
two 10-ounce packages
   frozen sweetened sliced
   strawberries, thawed, or
   2 cups sweetened sliced
   fresh strawberries
2 tablespoons orange
   liqueur
½ teaspoon salt
2 cups heavy cream
one 8-ounce store-bought
   jelly roll
additional strawberries and
   stiffly beaten heavy cream
   (optional)

1. Sprinkle gelatin over cold water in large heavy saucepan to soften. Drain ½ cup juice from thawed berries and add to gelatin in saucepan (or add ½ cup water to gelatin if using fresh berries); mix well.

2. Heat mixture over very low heat, stirring constantly, until gelatin is dissolved. Remove from heat and stir in strawberries, liqueur and salt. Chill until semi-set, 30 to 45 minutes.

3. Stiffly beat 2 cups cream. Fold into partially set gelatin.

4. Cut jelly roll into four or five ½-inch slices. Place slices upright around edge of 8-cup mold, 2-quart soufflé dish or 8-inch springform pan. Fill with strawberry mixture; chill until firm, about 4 hours.

5. At serving time, loosen edges of mold or springform pan with spatula; invert onto serving platter. Cover with hot dish towel for 1 minute; shake to release mold. Garnish with extra strawberries and beaten cream if desired.

CRUNCHI-FRUITTI ICE CREAM

1 half-gallon walnut or
   butter almond ice cream
⅓ cup finely chopped raisins
⅓ cup finely chopped
   candied cherries
⅓ cup grated sweetened
   chocolate or chocolate
   morsels
⅓ cup brandy
1 cup heavy cream
chocolate sprinkles and
   whole candied cherries

1. Turn ice cream into large bowl. Stir to soften, then quickly stir in raisins, chopped cherries, chocolate and brandy.

2. Immediately spoon into a 2-quart serving bowl. Freeze until firm, about 4 hours.

3. When ready to serve, stiffly beat heavy cream; spoon a ring of beaten cream around edge of dish. Garnish with chocolate sprinkles and whole candied cherries.

VALENTINE TEA

CURRY HAM ROLLS*

WATERCRESS
SANDWICHES

"ALL HEART"
CHEESECAKE*

SUGAR COOKIE HEARTS

CHERRY CAKELETS

VALENTINE CANDIES

SPICY NUT MIX*

TEA AND COFFEE

For eight.

WORK PLAN: Six hours before serving time or up to a day ahead, prepare "All Heart" Cheesecake (page 85); bake, chill and garnish with strawberries as directed. Make Spicy Nut Mix (page 85).

Three hours before serving time, prepare sugar cookie hearts by cutting one 14-ounce package refrigerator sugar cookie dough into slices as directed; cut into heart shapes with cookie cutter and bake according to label directions. To make cherry cakelets, prepare one 18.5-ounce package yellow cake mix according to label directions. Pour batter into 18 muffin liners in 3-inch muffin pans, filling half full. Bake according to label directions; cool in paper liners and top each with some cherry pie filling from one 20-ounce can.

Two hours before serving time, prepare Curry Ham Rolls (page 85). At the same time, make watercress sandwiches: Spread 16 slices thin whole wheat bread with softened butter or margarine; make filling by blending 1 cup finely chopped watercress with 2 to 3 tablespoons blue cheese salad dressing. Spread filling thinly over 8 buttered bread slices; top with remaining bread slices. Trim off crusts; cut each sandwich into fourths and wrap tightly in plastic wrap. Chill until serving time.

Serve a choice of tea or coffee and put out bowls of tiny sugar hearts.

CURRY HAM ROLLS

one 8-inch-long loaf French
  bread
1 tablespoon butter or
  margarine, softened
1 cup ground cooked ham,
  or one 6¾-ounce can
  deviled ham
2 tablespoons mayonnaise
1 tablespoon sweet pickle
  relish
¼ teaspoon curry powder
1 small tomato

1. Split loaf lengthwise in half; hollow out halves to make 2 "boats." Lightly butter insides of halves.

2. Mix ham, mayonnaise, relish and curry. Fill roll halves with ham mixture; wrap and chill.

3. To serve, cut each "boat" crosswise into bite-size slices. Arrange on plate with tomato rose garnish: Cut thick peel from tomato as though it were an apple. Roll tomato peel around finger to form rose; secure with half a toothpick.

"ALL HEART" CHEESECAKE

1 cup graham cracker
  crumbs
3 tablespoons butter or
  margarine, melted
two 8-ounce packages cream
  cheese
1 cup sugar
2 tablespoons lemon juice
1 teaspoon vanilla extract
¼ teaspoon salt
4 eggs
whole strawberries

1. Preheat oven to 325° F.

2. Thoroughly mix crumbs and melted butter or margarine. Press firmly on bottom and up sides of greased 4-cup heart-shaped gelatin mold or cake pan.

3. Using electric mixer at medium speed, beat cream cheese in large bowl until soft and smooth. Gradually blend in sugar, lemon juice, vanilla extract and salt. Add eggs one at a time, beating well after each addition.

4. Pour mixture into prepared mold or cake pan. Bake for 1 hour or until top puffs and is firm to the touch. Cool in pan on wire rack; cover and then chill. When ready to serve, loosen in mold and invert on plate. Surround with fresh whole strawberries.

SPICY NUT MIX

1 cup nuts (walnuts, pecans,
  almonds or a
  combination)
½ cup sugar
2 tablespoons butter or
  margarine
¼ teaspoon cinnamon
¼ teaspoon salt

1. In large heavy skillet, stir together nuts, sugar and butter or margarine. Place over medium heat and stir continuously for about 12 to 15 minutes, until sugar melts and nuts are coated with syrup.

2. Stir in cinnamon and salt. Spread on waxed paper to cool. *Makes 1 cup.*

Note: For variety, add ¼ cup raisins or pine nuts, or ½ cup coconut chips.

ST. PATRICK'S DAY SUPPER

HEARTY STEW*

COLESLAW

IRISH SODA BREAD*

BLARNEY STONES

LEPRESCONES

For six.

WORK PLAN: About 3 hours before serving time, prepare Hearty Stew (below). Then make coleslaw: Finely shred 1 small head cabbage; combine with 1 cup each grated carrot and apple. Toss with ½ cup each mayonnaise and sour cream, 1 tablespoon celery seed, 1½ teaspoons salt and ¼ teaspoon pepper; cover and chill until serving time. Two hours before serving time, prepare blarney stones and leprescones. For blarney stones, roll scoops of vanilla and chocolate ice cream in green-tinted coconut; freeze until serving time. For leprescones, make or buy brownies; frost with confectioners' sugar frosting tinted green and flavored with a drop or two of peppermint extract.

One hour before serving time, prepare Irish Soda Bread (page 87). Bake on top shelf set in upper third of oven, moving Hearty Stew to lower shelf of oven.

HEARTY STEW

2 tablespoons vegetable oil
2 pounds beef chuck, cut into cubes
2 cups diced peeled potatoes
2 cups sliced peeled carrots
one 10-ounce package frozen baby lima beans
one 10-ounce package frozen whole kernel corn
one 10-ounce package frozen cut green beans
1 cup chopped onion
1 clove garlic, crushed
1 tablespoon parsley flakes
three 8-ounce cans seasoned tomato sauce

1. Heat oil in large Dutch oven over medium heat; add beef cubes and sauté, turning to brown all sides. Add potatoes, carrots, lima beans, corn, green beans, onion, garlic and parsley. Pour tomato sauce over all.

2. Cover and bake at 350° F for 2 to 2½ hours, until meat is fork-tender. If necessary, add additional liquid such as broth, wine or water to keep stew juicy.

IRISH SODA BREAD

2 cups flour
2 tablespoons sugar
1½ teaspoons baking powder
½ teaspoon baking soda
3 tablespoons vegetable shortening, butter or margarine
1 cup buttermilk or sour milk
½ cup raisins

1. Preheat oven to 350° F.

2. In large bowl, mix flour, sugar, baking powder and baking soda. Using two knives or a pastry blender, cut in shortening, butter or margarine until mixture resembles coarse crumbs. Stir in milk; mix until all dry ingredients are moistened. Add raisins.

3. Gently knead dough on lightly floured board for several minutes, then shape into round loaf. Place loaf in greased 8-inch cake pan. Cut ¼-inch-deep cross in top. Bake for 40 to 50 minutes, until loaf sounds hollow when tapped on top. Turn out and cool on wire rack. *Makes 1 round loaf.*

EASTER LUNCH

ROAST LAMB WITH MINT JELLY

ASPARAGUS WITH HOLLANDAISE SAUCE

POTATO PUFF*

APRICOT ASPIC*

MERINGUE BRICKLE CAKE*

For six.

WORK PLAN: The day before, prepare Meringue Brickle Cake (page 89). At the same time, make Apricot Aspic (page 88); unmold and make dressing as directed just before serving time.

Two to 2½ hours before serving time, place one 5- to 6-pound leg of lamb on rack in roasting pan; rub surfaces with ¼ cup olive oil, then a mixture of 1 tablespoon each crushed rosemary and thyme, 2 teaspoons salt and ¼ teaspoon pepper. Roast lamb at 375° F for 1 hour and 20 minutes to 1 hour and 50 minutes. Baste frequently with pan juices and additional oil. Serve with mint jelly.

Thirty minutes before serving time, make Potato Puff (page 88). About 15 minutes before serving, wash and peel 3 pounds fresh asparagus and cook in large skillet in ½ inch boiling salted water until crisp-tender (or cook four 10-ounce packages frozen asparagus spears according to label directions). Prepare hollandaise sauce by combining ¾ cup each sour cream and mayonnaise in top of double boiler over hot (not boiling) water; add 2 egg yolks, 2 tablespoons lemon juice and 2 teaspoons grated lemon rind. Heat until very hot, stirring frequently. Serve over drained asparagus.

POTATO PUFF

2 cups instant mashed
   potato flakes
unflavored yogurt or sour
   cream
1 egg, beaten
1 tablespoon butter or
   margarine
1 tablespoon snipped chives
½ cup grated sharp Cheddar
   cheese

1. Preheat oven to 375° F.

2. Prepare instant mashed potatoes in medium saucepan according to label directions, substituting yogurt or sour cream for the milk. Mix in beaten egg.

3. Turn into greased 1½-quart casserole; dot with butter or margarine and sprinkle with chives and grated cheese. Bake for 20 to 25 minutes, until browned and bubbly.

APRICOT ASPIC

2 cups apricot nectar
1 tablespoon lemon juice
2 sticks cinnamon
1 teaspoon whole cloves
one 6-ounce package
   apricot-flavored gelatin
2 cups cold water
watercress
1 tablespoon grated orange
   rind

DRESSING
⅓ cup mayonnaise
⅓ cup unflavored yogurt

1. In medium saucepan, mix nectar, lemon juice, cinnamon and cloves; bring to boiling point. Reduce heat to low and simmer for 5 minutes.

2. Stir apricot gelatin into hot liquid until gelatin is completely dissolved. Stir in cold water.

3. Rinse 4- or 5-cup mold with cold water. Strain gelatin mixture into rinsed mold. Chill overnight or until firm.

4. To serve, loosen mold around edges with sharp knife; quickly dip mold into hot water; invert onto bed of watercress on serving platter and sprinkle with orange rind. To make dressing, mix mayonnaise and yogurt; serve alongside aspic.

Note: If desired, make a more substantial Apricot Aspic by adding apricots from one 16-ounce can. Drain the apricot halves and cut them in half again. Follow the above recipe through Step 3, but chill the gelatin mixture only until syrupy, about 30 minutes. Stir in the drained cut-up apricots, then chill the aspic and serve as directed.

MERINGUE BRICKLE CAKE

10 egg whites
1 tablespoon white vinegar
⅛ teaspoon salt
3 cups sugar
1 teaspoon vanilla extract
3 cups heavy cream
2 tablespoons sugar
½ teaspoon vanilla extract
⅓ cup brickle or peanut
  brittle, finely crushed

1. Preheat oven to 300° F. Grease two 9-inch cake pans. Cut circles of waxed paper to fit into bottoms of pans; grease paper.

2. Using electric mixer at high speed, beat egg whites in large bowl until frothy. Add vinegar and salt; beat until soft peaks form. Add 3 cups sugar in thin stream, beating continuously. Add 1 teaspoon vanilla extract; beat whites until stiff.

3. Divide meringue between prepared pans and spread evenly. Bake for 45 minutes. Turn off oven; leave meringue in oven 25 minutes longer. Turn out on wire rack; peel off paper. Turn top side up; cool completely.

4. Beat cream with 2 tablespoons sugar and ½ teaspoon vanilla extract until stiff.

5. To assemble cake, place 1 meringue layer on serving plate; spread with generous layer of beaten cream. Spread brickle or peanut brittle over beaten cream and top with second meringue layer. Frost cake with remaining beaten cream. Refrigerate for up to 24 hours. *Makes one 9-inch layer cake.*

GRADUATION PARTY

PINEAPPLE SANGRIA
PUNCH*

GRETCHEN'S TACO
SALAD*

CHILI CORN BREAD*

MELON AND
STRAWBERRY ICE CREAM
DESSERT*

DIPLOMA COOKIES*

For ten to twelve.

WORK PLAN: At least 4 hours before serving time or the day before, do first step of Melon and Strawberry Ice Cream Dessert and make Diploma Cookies (page 91). Prepare Pineapple Sangria Punch (page 90); just before serving, add ginger ale or soda and garnish.

Two hours before serving time, prepare Gretchen's Taco Salad (page 90); cover and chill, and toss with dressing just before serving.

One hour before serving time, prepare fruit for Melon and Strawberry Ice Cream Dessert as directed. Finish dessert when ready to serve.

Thirty minutes before serving, prepare Chili Corn Bread (page 91); serve warm.

PINEAPPLE SANGRIA PUNCH

3 cups pineapple juice
3 cups cranberry juice
⅔ cup sugar
2 trays ice cubes
two 28-ounce bottles ginger
   ale or soda water
1 orange, thinly sliced
1 lemon, thinly sliced

1. In large pitcher, mix pineapple juice, cranberry juice, sugar and 1 tray of the ice cubes. Stir until sugar dissolves. Chill for several hours.

2. At serving time, pour juice mixture into large punch bowl over second tray of ice cubes. Stir in ginger ale or soda. Garnish with orange and lemon slices. *Makes 4 quarts.*

GRETCHEN'S TACO SALAD

2 pounds lean ground beef
2 teaspoons chili powder
2 teaspoons salt
6 drops hot pepper sauce
1 large head iceberg lettuce
1 cup thinly sliced onion
one 15-ounce can pinto
   beans, rinsed and drained
3 cups shredded sharp
   Cheddar cheese
1 cup sliced pitted ripe
   olives
2 tomatoes, cut into small
   wedges
1 large or 2 small ripe
   avocados, pitted, peeled
   and diced
1 cup coarsely crushed
   tortilla chips

DRESSING
½ cup creamy French
   dressing
½ cup unflavored yogurt

pepitas (salted pumpkin
   seeds)

1. Brown ground beef in large skillet over medium heat. Drain excess fat from skillet. Stir chili powder, salt and hot pepper sauce into beef; set mixture aside.

2. Chop or shred lettuce; separate onion slices into rings. In very large salad bowl, layer lettuce, onion rings, pinto beans, reserved cooked meat mixture, half of cheese, the olives, tomatoes, diced avocados, crushed tortilla chips and remaining cheese. Chill until serving time.

3. Just before serving, mix together French dressing and yogurt; pour over salad and toss. Accompany salad with bowl of pepitas for sprinkling to taste.

CHILI CORN BREAD

one 8-ounce package corn
   muffin mix
one 4-ounce can chopped
   green chilies, drained
3 tablespoons butter or
   margarine, melted

1. Preheat oven to 400° F.

2. Prepare corn muffin mix according to label directions; turn batter into greased 15 x 10 x 1-inch jelly-roll pan, spreading evenly. Sprinkle batter with drained chopped chilies; drizzle with melted butter or margarine.

3. Bake for 20 to 25 minutes, until browned and firm. Cut into squares to serve.

MELON AND STRAWBERRY ICE CREAM DESSERT

1 quart lemon or vanilla ice
   cream
1 large ripe honeydew
   melon
1 quart ripe strawberries
¼ cup sugar
juice and grated rind of
   1 large navel orange
fresh mint (optional)

1. Stir ice cream to soften; pack into 4- or 5-cup mold. Store in freezer for several hours or overnight, until firm.

2. About 1 hour before serving time, peel, seed and dice melon; wash and hull strawberries; place in large bowl. Sprinkle sugar and orange juice and rind over fruit. Stir gently to melt sugar. Arrange fruit around edge of 12-inch rimmed serving platter.

3. At serving time, dip ice cream mold into hot water; unmold ice cream in center of fruit-filled platter. Garnish with fresh mint if desired.

DIPLOMA COOKIES

¾ cup brown sugar, firmly
   packed
⅓ cup butter or margarine
2 tablespoons flour
2 tablespoons milk
2 teaspoons vanilla extract
1¼ cups old-fashioned
   rolled oats

1. Preheat oven to 350° F.

2. In large bowl, cream together brown sugar and butter or margarine. Beat in flour, milk and vanilla extract. Mix in oats until thoroughly blended.

3. Drop batter by teaspoonfuls onto greased baking sheets, arranging 6 teaspoonfuls to a sheet, 2 inches apart.

4. Bake for 10 minutes, until cookies are spread and browned. Cool on sheet for a few seconds, then use spatula to turn cookies over and roll up into little cylinders, rolling over handle of a wooden spoon. Cool completely on wire rack, then tie with ribbon to look like little diplomas. *Makes about 24.*

FOURTH OF JULY PARTY

SALMON IN PUFF
PASTRY*

GRILLED STEAK AND
CHICKEN

NEW PEAS AND
POTATOES

GARDEN LETTUCE SALAD

FIRECRACKER SUNDAES*·

BLUEBERRY CRISP PIE*

For six.

WORK PLAN: About 4 hours before serving time, prepare ice cream and topping for Firecracker Sundaes (page 93); assemble at dessert time. At the same time, prepare garden lettuce salad by tossing 8 cups small lettuce leaves, 2 cups each tomato wedges and cucumbers and ½ cup each black and green olives, halved, in large salad bowl; cover and chill. At serving time, toss with ¾ cup blue cheese dressing.

One and a quarter hours before serving time, prepare Blueberry Crisp Pie (page 93) and Salmon in Puff Pastry (below).

About 25 minutes before serving time, wash 2 pounds new potatoes and peel center band from each; cook in boiling salted water to cover in very large saucepan until tender, about 15 minutes. About 5 minutes before end of cooking time, add 2 pounds fresh shelled peas or one 32-ounce polybag frozen peas. Drain, and toss with ½ cup each butter or margarine and chopped mint or parsley.

Ten to 20 minutes before serving time, broil one 1½-pound sirloin steak 4 inches from heat for 4 to 10 minutes per side; broil 6 boneless chicken breast halves for 4 minutes per side. Baste steak and chicken with ½ cup Italian-style salad dressing.

SALMON IN PUFF PASTRY

**3 or 4 frozen patty shells,
    thawed
one 16-ounce can salmon,
    drained
1 tablespoon butter or
    margarine
¼ cup finely chopped onion
2 hard-cooked eggs, sliced
2 tablespoons chopped
    parsley
¾ teaspoon salt
¼ teaspoon dried dill
¼ teaspoon pepper
1 egg, beaten**

1. Preheat oven to 400° F.

2. On floured board or pastry cloth, overlap edges of thawed patty shells and press firmly together to make one piece. Roll out pastry to make a 12 x 11-inch rectangle. Place pastry on baking sheet.

3. Flake drained salmon, removing bones and skin. Spread down center of pastry rectangle.

4. Melt butter or margarine in small skillet over medium heat; add onion and sauté until tender, about 4 minutes. Spoon onion over salmon. Spread egg slices over salmon and onion; sprinkle with parsley, salt, dill and pepper.

5. Moisten edges of pastry; bring up and overlap to completely enclose filling on all sides. Press edges firmly together. If desired, shape roll into a fish, forming tail at one end, head at the other; make scale marks with tip of teaspoon. Brush with beaten egg.

6. Bake for 30 minutes. Serve hot, cut in thin slices.

Note: A 1-pound piece of fresh salmon, boiled, skinned and flaked, may be used instead of the canned salmon.

FIRECRACKER SUNDAES

6 large scoops of vanilla ice cream
1 pint fresh blueberries
1 pint fresh strawberries, hulled and halved

1. Place 1 ice cream ball in each of 6 parfait or sundae glasses; store in freezer until serving time.

2. Mix blueberries and strawberries; spoon over ice cream. Serve at once.

BLUEBERRY CRISP PIE

one 9- to 11-ounce package piecrust mix

FILLING
4 cups fresh or frozen (and thawed) blueberries
1 cup sugar
¼ cup flour
2 tablespoons butter or margarine

TOPPING
¾ cup flour
½ cup sugar
¼ teaspoon cinnamon
⅓ cup butter or margarine

1. Preheat oven to 400° F.

2. Prepare piecrust mix according to label directions. Divide in half; wrap and refrigerate one portion for another use. Roll out remaining half to line 9-inch pie plate; trim and flute edge.

3. To make filling, toss blueberries with 1 cup sugar and ¼ cup flour. Place in pie shell; dot with 2 tablespoons butter or margarine.

4. To make topping, combine ¾ cup flour, ½ cup sugar and the cinnamon in small bowl. Cut in ⅓ cup butter or margarine until crumbly. Sprinkle over filling. Bake for 40 minutes, until topping is crisp and filling is bubbly.

HALLOWEEN PARTY

BAKED HAM

CURRIED DRIED FRUIT COMPOTE*

CREAMY MOLASSES LIMA BEANS*

TOSSED ROMAINE SALAD

JACK-O'-LANTERN DESSERT*

GINGERSNAPS*

For six.

WORK PLAN: About 3 hours before serving time, prepare Gingersnaps (page 95).

About 2 hours before serving, prepare ham: Trim outer fat from a 5-pound ready-to-eat ham butt, leaving ½-inch layer; score fat left on ham into diamond shapes. Bake at 350° F for 1½ to 2 hours or until meat thermometer registers 180° F, basting during last 45 minutes of cooking time with melted apricot preserves from one 10-ounce jar. At the same time, make Curried Dried Fruit Compote (below); bake with ham. Then prepare Creamy Molasses Lima Beans (page 95); bake alongside fruit compote.

One hour before serving time, prepare Jack-o'-Lantern Dessert (page 95); freeze until serving time. At the same time, place 6 cups bite-size pieces romaine in salad bowl; cover and chill, and toss with ⅓ cup Caesar salad dressing just before serving.

CURRIED DRIED FRUIT COMPOTE

two 11-ounce packages mixed dried fruit
2 cups water
½ cup brown sugar, firmly packed
1 to 2 tablespoons curry powder
1 strip orange rind
1 strip lemon rind

1. Place mixed dried fruit in 2-quart casserole. In small saucepan, combine water, brown sugar, curry, orange rind and lemon rind. Heat over low heat, stirring, until sugar is dissolved.

2. Pour curry mixture over dried fruit. Cover casserole tightly and bake at 350° F for 1½ to 2 hours, until fruit is tender and mixture is bubbly.

CREAMY MOLASSES LIMA BEANS

**two 16-ounce cans large
  lima beans, drained**
1 cup sour cream
**2 tablespoons dark
  molasses**
1½ teaspoons dry mustard
¼ cup butter or margarine

1. Place drained lima beans in greased 2-quart casserole.

2. Mix sour cream, molasses and dry mustard; stir into beans. Dot with butter or margarine. Bake at 350° F for about 1 hour, until crusty and browned.

JACK-O'-LANTERN DESSERT

6 large oranges
**1 quart butterscotch ripple
  or butter pecan ice cream**
whole cloves

1. Using sharp paring knife, cut off tops of oranges about one-third of the way down (zigzag or straight as desired). Remove orange pulp; reserve for another use.

2. Fill orange shells with large scoops of ice cream, mounding it high. Replace orange caps.

3. Insert whole cloves in sides of oranges to make eyes and mouths. Serve at once or freeze until ready to serve.

GINGERSNAPS

4 cups flour
½ cup sugar
1 teaspoon ginger
½ teaspoon salt
¼ teaspoon nutmeg
**1 cup vegetable shortening,
  butter or margarine**
1 teaspoon baking soda
1 tablespoon hot water
1 cup dark or light molasses
additional sugar

1. In large bowl, mix flour, ½ cup sugar, the ginger, salt and nutmeg. Using two knives or a pastry blender, cut in shortening, butter or margarine until mixture is crumbly.

2. Dissolve baking soda in hot water; stir into molasses. Make a well in center of flour-shortening mixture and add molasses mixture all at once; mix very well.

3. Divide cookie dough in half; shape each dough half into 8 x 2-inch log. Wrap in waxed paper and chill for at least 1 hour, until firm.

4. Preheat oven to 350° F.

5. Cut logs into ¼-inch-thick rounds; arrange on ungreased baking sheets and sprinkle with sugar. Bake for 5 to 7 minutes, just until edges begin to darken. Cool on baking sheets on wire rack for 2 to 3 minutes; remove from sheets to rack and cool completely. *Makes about 60.*

THANKSGIVING DINNER

BOUILLON BISQUE*

GLAZED TURKEY WITH
GIBLET GRAVY AND
APPLE-SAUSAGE
STUFFING*

TOASTY CHESTNUT
STUFFING*

SQUASH WITH
CRANBERRIES*

RELISH TRAY

CREAMED ONIONS

GREEN BEANS

MASHED POTATOES

CRUMPKIN PIE*

CREAM-TOPPED
CRAN-MINCE TARTS*

FALL FRUITCAKE*

For ten to twelve.

WORK PLAN: Up to 2 weeks in advance, make Cranberry Relish (page 99) and store in refrigerator. Up to 1 week ahead, make Great Piecrust (page 105) and store as directed.

A day ahead of time, make Crumpkin Pie, Cream-Topped Cran-Mince Tarts and Fall Fruitcake (pages 100 and 105). Serve all three as dessert choice at end of Thanksgiving dinner, reheating pie and tarts just before serving if desired. Vegetables for relish tray, the silverskin onions and green beans can be washed and/or peeled and stored a day ahead of time in separate plastic bags in the refrigerator. Soak chestnuts for Toasty Chestnut Stuffing overnight (see recipe page 99).

Five hours before serving dinner, prepare Glazed Turkey with Giblet Gravy, stuffing it with Apple-Sausage Stuffing (pages 97–98). Prepare Squash with Cranberries (page 99); bake with turkey. Make Toasty Chestnut Stuffing (page 99) to serve as a side dish. Arrange 1 bunch cleaned celery stalks, 2 packages cleaned radishes, one 12-ounce jar stuffed olives, drained, one 12-ounce jar black olives, drained, and one 8-ounce jar gherkins, drained, on large relish tray; wrap and refrigerate until serving time.

About 40 minutes before serving time, boil 4 pounds peeled silverskin onions in salted water to cover for about 15 to 20 minutes, until tender; drain. Make a white sauce by melting ¾ cup butter or margarine in medium saucepan over low heat; blend in ¾ cup flour and cook for 2 minutes. Blend in 4 cups milk; bring to boiling point, stirring constantly, and season with salt and pepper to taste. Add cooked onions; heat for 10 minutes before serving.

Meanwhile, wash and peel 4 pounds potatoes; cut into apricot-size pieces. Boil in salted water to cover for about 20 minutes, until tender; drain. Using electric mixer at medium speed, beat potatoes until smooth, adding ½ cup hot milk, ½ cup butter or margarine, 1 teaspoon salt and ½ teaspoon each pepper and nutmeg. Cook 4 pounds washed and trimmed green beans in boiling salted water to cover for about 8 to 10 minutes, until just tender; drain, and toss with ½ cup butter or margarine just before serving. Prepare Bouillon Bisque (below).

BOUILLON BISQUE

two 11-ounce cans
  condensed tomato bisque
6 beef bouillon cubes
6 soup cans water
½ teaspoon crumbled
  rosemary
2 to 3 drops hot pepper
  sauce
½ cup dry sherry
croutons

1. In large saucepan, mix condensed tomato bisque, bouillon cubes, water, rosemary and hot pepper sauce; heat to boiling point.

2. Reduce heat to low and simmer, stirring, until bouillon cubes are completely dissolved. Just before serving, stir in sherry and float croutons on top. Serve in mugs, soup bowls or bisque cups.

GLAZED TURKEY WITH GIBLET GRAVY

Apple-Sausage Stuffing
  (page 98)
12- to 15-pound turkey
butter or margarine,
  softened
salt and pepper

APPLE GLAZE
1 cup apple juice
2 tablespoons brown sugar

Giblet Gravy (page 98)

1. Prepare Apple-Sausage Stuffing. Wash turkey under cold running water; pat dry with paper towels.

2. Fill neck cavity with 1½ to 2 cups Apple-Sausage Stuffing. Fasten neck skin to back of bird with a skewer. Fill body cavity loosely with stuffing; skewer or sew closed. (Place any extra stuffing in greased baking dish; bake beside turkey for last 30 minutes of roasting time.)

3. Place stuffed turkey breast side up in roasting pan. Rub all over with butter or margarine. Sprinkle with salt and pepper. Tent loosely with foil. Roast at 325° F for 3 to 3½ hours, basting frequently.

4. Meanwhile, make apple glaze by combining apple juice and brown sugar in small saucepan. Stir over low heat until sugar dissolves. Remove foil from turkey and spoon glaze over turkey. Roast 1 hour longer, basting frequently with pan drippings.

5. Meanwhile, make Giblet Gravy. Remove turkey from pan to warm platter. Bird will slice better if allowed to stand for about 15 to 20 minutes before carving. Serve with Giblet Gravy.

Apple-Sausage Stuffing

12 cups day-old white bread
  cubes
¼ cup butter or margarine
1 pound mildly seasoned
  bulk sausage meat
1½ cups chopped onions
1½ cups sliced celery
1½ cups chopped apples
½ cup raisins
1 cup apple juice
1½ teaspoons thyme
1½ teaspoons crumbled
  rosemary
1 teaspoon sage
1½ teaspoons salt
pepper to taste

1. Spread bread cubes in shallow baking pan; toast in preheating oven until crisp and dry, about 10 minutes.

2. Melt butter or margarine in large skillet over medium heat; add sausage meat and brown, stirring with spoon or fork to break meat into small pieces. Stir in onions, celery, apples and raisins; cook for a few minutes, until tender. Add apple juice and mix well. Stir in thyme, rosemary, sage, salt and pepper.

3. In large mixing bowl, combine bread cubes and sausage mixture. Toss lightly, until completely mixed. *Makes approximately 15 to 16 cups.*

Giblet Gravy

giblets and neck of 1 turkey
1 small onion
water to cover
water, vegetable cooking
  liquid or chicken broth
¾ cup flour
salt and pepper to taste

1. Place giblets, neck and onion in medium saucepan with water to cover; bring to boiling point. Reduce heat to medium, and simmer until giblets are tender, 45 to 60 minutes; add additional water as needed to keep giblets covered. Remove and reserve giblets and neck; discard onion.

2. After placing Glazed Turkey (above) on warm platter, skim fat from drippings in roasting pan; reserve fat. Pour liquid from pan into giblet broth. Add enough water, vegetable cooking liquid or chicken broth to measure 6 cups giblet broth.

3. Return 2 to 3 tablespoons reserved fat to roasting pan. Add flour, stirring until smooth. Gradually stir in hot broth. Place pan over low heat. Stir constantly, scraping up brown particles, until gravy thickens. Strain gravy into saucepan.

4. Finely chop giblets and neck meat and stir into gravy. Add salt and pepper. Keep hot over low heat until ready to serve. *Makes approximately 8 cups.*

TOASTY CHESTNUT STUFFING

½ pound chestnuts
salt
one 16-ounce package herb
  stuffing mix

1. Place chestnuts in medium saucepan; add warm water to cover. Cover pan and let stand overnight. Drain.

2. Cover soaked chestnuts with boiling water; add a sprinkle of salt. Cover pan and boil for 1 hour, adding more water as needed to keep chestnuts covered. Drain and cool. Shell and peel chestnuts; chop coarsely.

3. Prepare stuffing mix according to label directions. Add chestnuts and toss lightly.

4. Spread stuffing in greased 12 x 8 x 2-inch baking dish. Bake in 325° F oven with turkey for last 30 minutes of roasting time.

SQUASH WITH CRANBERRIES

3 medium acorn squash
¼ cup butter or margarine
¼ cup brown sugar, firmly
  packed
salt to taste
Cranberry Relish (below)

1. Cut squash in half; scrape out seeds and fiber. Cut each squash half into two pieces.

2. Place squash pieces skin side down in lightly greased 13 x 9 x 2-inch baking dish. Dot with butter or margarine; sprinkle with brown sugar and salt.

3. Cover dish with foil. Bake at 325° F for 1 to 1¼ hours, until tender. At serving time, spoon Cranberry Relish over and around squash. Serve extra relish alongside.

Cranberry Relish

1 pound fresh or frozen
  (and thawed) cranberries
4 small tangerines or
  kumquats
1½ to 2 cups sugar

1. Rinse cranberries; discard stems and soft berries. Put berries through food grinder using medium blade, or grind in food processor.

2. Peel tangerines or kumquats and remove fiber from white part of skin. Put rind and fruit segments through food grinder or food processor and add to cranberries.

3. Stir sugar into ground fruit mixture. Mix well and let stand until sugar is completely dissolved. Refrigerate until ready to serve. Relish will keep for 2 weeks. *Makes approximately 6 cups.*

CRUMPKIN PIE

1½ cups canned pumpkin
¾ cup sugar
1 teaspoon cinnamon
½ teaspoon salt
½ teaspoon ginger
¼ teaspoon nutmeg
¼ teaspoon cloves
3 eggs
1½ cups milk
⅔ cup evaporated milk
one 9-inch unbaked pie shell
  (see Great Piecrust recipe
  page 105)

TOPPING
2 tablespoons butter or
  margarine, softened
¼ cup sugar
¼ cup flour
¼ teaspoon cinnamon
1 tablespoon finely chopped
  or ground pecans

1. Preheat oven to 400° F.

2. In large bowl, mix pumpkin, ¾ cup sugar, 1 teaspoon cinnamon, the salt, ginger, nutmeg and cloves. Add eggs one at a time, beating after each addition. Stir in milk and evaporated milk.

3. Make sure pie shell has a high crimped edge to hold all the filling. Slide oven rack partway out; place pie shell in center of rack. Pour filling carefully into shell; slide rack back into oven slowly to prevent spilling. Bake for 40 minutes.

4. Meanwhile, make topping by thoroughly mixing butter or margarine, ¼ cup sugar, the flour, ¼ teaspoon cinnamon and the pecans to make a crumbly mixture. Carefully spread crumb topping on baked pie.

5. Return pie to oven and bake 10 to 15 minutes longer, until top is crisp and knife inserted in center comes out clean. Cool, then chill before serving.

CREAM-TOPPED CRAN-MINCE TARTS

2¼ cups prepared
  mincemeat
1 cup fresh cranberries,
  chopped
twelve 3-inch unbaked tart
  shells (see Great Piecrust
  recipe page 105)
1 egg
1 cup sour cream
1 tablespoon sugar
1 tablespoon rum or brandy

1. Preheat oven to 400° F.

2. Mix 2 cups of the mincemeat and the chopped cranberries. Spoon mixture into tart shells. Bake for 20 to 25 minutes, until crust is nicely browned.

3. Meanwhile, thoroughly combine egg, sour cream, sugar and rum or brandy. Spoon 1 tablespoon mixture onto each tart. Return to oven and bake 6 to 8 minutes longer, until filling is bubbly. Cool. Garnish each tart with 1 teaspoon remaining mincemeat.

Christmas Dinner (*pages 106 through 109*)

East/West Buffet (*pages 76 through 78*)

Sixteenth Birthday Party (*pages 114 through 116*)

French Apple Tart (*page 120*)

Great Piecrust

5 cups flour
1 tablespoon sugar
2 teaspoons salt
2 cups shortening
1 egg
approximately ¾ cup cold
  water

1. In large bowl, mix flour, sugar and salt. Using two knives or a pastry blender, cut shortening into flour mixture until mixture resembles coarse cornmeal.

2. Beat egg in measuring cup; add enough cold water to measure 1 cup liquid. Add liquid to flour mixture; stir until dough leaves sides of bowl and forms a ball.

3. Divide dough into 3 equal pieces; wrap each tightly in plastic wrap. Refrigerate for up to 1 week (or freeze for up to 3 months and thaw overnight in refrigerator when ready to use). Roll out on floured board to ⅛-inch thickness. *Makes enough for three 8- or 9-inch pie shells, or twelve to fourteen 3-inch tart shells.*

FALL FRUITCAKE

½ cup butter or margarine
1½ cups granulated sugar
2 eggs
2 cups flour
1 teaspoon baking soda
½ teaspoon baking powder
¼ teaspoon salt
1 cup mashed ripe banana
¼ cup sour milk or apple
  cider
½ cup raisins
1 apple, peeled and chopped
1 tablespoon flour
1 teaspoon vanilla extract

GLAZE
1 cup confectioners' sugar
2 tablespoons apple cider

1. Preheat oven to 325° F. Grease and flour 10-inch tube pan or large bundt pan.

2. In large bowl, cream butter or margarine until soft and smooth. Add granulated sugar, about ½ cup at a time, beating after each addition until mixture is fluffy. Beat in eggs one at a time.

3. Sift 2 cups flour, the baking soda, baking powder and salt onto waxed paper. Add dry ingredients alternately with mashed banana and ¼ cup sour milk or cider to creamed mixture. Beat until smooth and creamy.

4. Toss raisins and chopped apple with 1 tablespoon flour; stir into batter along with vanilla extract.

5. Spoon batter into prepared pan. Bake for 35 to 45 minutes, until cake tester inserted in center comes out clean. Cool in pan on wire rack for 10 minutes; invert onto rack and cool completely.

6. Meanwhile, make glaze by mixing together confectioners' sugar and 2 tablespoons cider. Spread over cooled cake. *Makes one 10-inch tube or bundt cake.*

CHRISTMAS DINNER

HOLIDAY RIB ROAST
WITH
OVEN-BROWNED
POTATOES*

GREEN VEGETABLE
CASSEROLE*

CHERRY BURGUNDY
RING*

PLUM DUFF*

AUNT BESS'S LEMON
CHESS PIE*

DATE-NUT
CONFECTIONS*

MINTS

For eight to ten.

WORK PLAN: A day or two ahead of time, make Plum Duff, Aunt Bess's Lemon Chess Pie and Date-Nut Confections (pages 108–109). Carefully follow storage, reheating and additional serving instructions. Serve all three as dessert choice at the end of Christmas dinner, passing after-dinner mints as well.

At least 6 hours before serving time, make Cherry Burgundy Ring (page 107). Prepare Holiday Rib Roast (below); calculate according to the recipe how long the meat will take to cook, and prepare Oven-Browned Potatoes and Green Vegetable Casserole (page 107) accordingly. Bake casserole alongside rib roast. *Pictured on page 101.*

HOLIDAY RIB ROAST WITH OVEN-BROWNED POTATOES

2- to 3-rib standing rib roast
coarsely ground black
pepper
1 cup packaged crushed
herb stuffing mix
1 bay leaf, crushed
2 tablespoons butter or
margarine, softened
Oven-Browned Potatoes
(page 107)

1. Preheat oven to 325° F.

2. Place rib roast fat side up on wire rack in roasting pan. Sprinkle with a little black pepper.

3. Combine stuffing mix and crushed bay leaf. Press mixture into fat side of beef. Spread butter or margarine over the cut meat surfaces. Place in oven and roast, allowing 18 to 20 minutes per pound for rare; 22 to 25 minutes for medium; 27 to 30 minutes for well done. Serve with Oven-Browned Potatoes.

Oven-Browned Potatoes

5 or 6 medium potatoes
1 small onion, halved
2 teaspoons salt

1. Peel and halve potatoes. Place in saucepan; add onion, salt and water to cover. Bring to boiling point; boil for 10 minutes. Drain potatoes and discard onion.

2. Place potatoes in drippings around beef for last 45 minutes of roasting time. Using long-handled spoon, turn potatoes several times to brown evenly.

GREEN VEGETABLE CASSEROLE

three 10-ounce packages frozen green vegetables (a combination of peas, broccoli and cut green beans; or lima beans, spinach and artichokes)
3 tablespoons butter or margarine
½ cup chopped onion
3 tablespoons flour
2 cups milk
1 tablespoon ketchup
3 to 4 drops hot pepper sauce
salt and pepper to taste
1 cup grated longhorn or mild Cheddar cheese

1. Cook frozen green vegetables according to package directions, reducing suggested cooking time by 2 or 3 minutes so vegetables remain crisp. Drain vegetables; turn into greased 12 x 8 x 2-inch baking dish.

2. Melt butter or margarine in medium skillet over medium heat; add onion and sauté for 4 minutes, until tender. Blend in flour; cook and stir for about 1 minute, until bubbly. Slowly add milk, stirring constantly. Add ketchup and hot pepper sauce. Continue to stir until mixture thickens. Season with salt and pepper.

3. Pour sauce over vegetables in baking dish. Sprinkle cheese over vegetables. Bake at 350° F for 45 minutes, until top is browned and bubbly.

CHERRY BURGUNDY RING

one 6-ounce package wild cherry-flavored gelatin
1½ cups water
½ cup red Burgundy wine
one 16-ounce can tart pitted cherries, drained
one 29-ounce can apricot halves, drained and cut in half

DRESSING
2 cups unflavored yogurt
2 tablespoons honey
⅛ teaspoon nutmeg

curly endive

1. Prepare gelatin according to label directions, using 1½ cups water and ½ cup wine to make 2 cups liquid. Chill until mixture is consistency of unbeaten egg whites, about 30 minutes.

2. Stir drained cherries and apricots into thickened gelatin. Pour mixture into lightly oiled 6-cup ring mold. Chill for several hours, until set.

3. Meanwhile, make dressing by stirring yogurt to creamy consistency; stir in honey and nutmeg. To unmold gelatin, loosen mold around edges with sharp knife; quickly dip mold into hot water. Invert onto bed of curly endive on serving platter. Serve dressing alongside.

PLUM DUFF

4 cups fine dry bread
  crumbs
4 cups flour
2 cups sugar
1 tablespoon cinnamon
1 teaspoon salt
1 teaspoon nutmeg
2 pounds beef suet, trimmed
  of membrane and
  chopped
one 16-ounce box seeded
  muscat raisins
one 16-ounce box golden
  raisins
2 cups chopped dried apples
  or fresh tart apples
12 eggs
grated rind and juice of
  2 medium lemons
½ cup brandy
1 cup sweet cider or apple
  juice
hard sauce

1. In extra-large bowl, combine bread crumbs, flour, sugar, cinnamon, salt and nutmeg. Mix until well blended. Mix in chopped suet, both kinds of raisins and the apples.

2. In another large bowl, beat eggs until frothy. Beat in lemon rind and juice, brandy and cider or apple juice.

3. Add egg mixture to suet-raisin mixture. Mix until all dry ingredients are moistened and thoroughly incorporated into batter.

4. Fill 2 well-greased 8-cup pudding molds and four well-greased 1-pound coffee cans about two-thirds full of batter. Cover top of each mold with parchment paper or heavy-duty waxed paper, firmly securing with string or rubber band.

5. Place molds on wire rack in kettle containing about 3 inches hot water. Cover kettle; steam pudding over low heat for 3 hours. Add water as needed.

6. Uncover molds and completely cool pudding in molds on wire racks. Wipe molds dry and re-cover with clean waxed paper and heavy-duty aluminum foil. Store in refrigerator or in cool, dry, dark place until ready to serve.

7. To serve hot, steam in molds for 1 hour, or wrap unmolded pudding tightly in aluminum foil and reheat in 325° F oven for 1 hour. Serve with hard sauce.

Note: Recipe can easily be cut in half to fill 1 large mold or several smaller molds.

AUNT BESS'S LEMON CHESS PIE

1¾ cups sugar
1 tablespoon flour
1 tablespoon cornmeal
⅛ teaspoon salt
4 eggs
¼ cup butter or margarine,
  melted
2 tablespoons dried or
  freshly grated lemon rind
¼ cup lemon juice
one 9-inch unbaked pie shell
  (see Great Piecrust recipe,
  page 105)
chopped candied cherries

1. Preheat oven to 350° F.

2. In large bowl, thoroughly mix sugar, flour, cornmeal and salt. Beat in eggs one at a time. Add melted butter or margarine, lemon rind and lemon juice; mix well.

3. Pour mixture into unbaked pie shell. Bake for 35 to 40 minutes, until knife inserted in center comes out clean. Cool on wire rack, then chill until ready to serve. Garnish with chopped candied cherries.

Note: To make Coconut Chess Pie, substitute ⅓ cup grated fresh coconut for the lemon rind, and ¼ cup coconut milk for the lemon juice; add ½ teaspoon vanilla extract.

DATE-NUT CONFECTIONS

¾ cup light corn syrup
3 cups sugar
½ cup evaporated milk
one 16-ounce package
   snipped dates
½ cup broken pecans

1. In large heavy saucepan, combine corn syrup, sugar and evaporated milk; mix well. Cook over medium heat, stirring to dissolve sugar. Cook to soft ball stage (240° F on candy thermometer).

2. Remove from heat. Beat in dates and pecans. Cool for a few minutes, then pour candy mixture down the middle of 15 x 10 x 1-inch jelly-roll pan lined with damp piece of muslin.

3. As candy cools, shape it into a log by pushing with rubber scraper. When completely cooled, wrap in waxed paper and store in a tightly covered tin or overwrap in heavy-duty aluminum foil and store in refrigerator. To serve, cut into thin slices.

BIRTHDAY FETE

SHRIMP WITH PEPPERS *

PARSLIED RICE

BAKED BUTTERED
SQUASH *

BIBB LETTUCE SALAD

BURNT SUGAR CAKE *

For four.

WORK PLAN: At least 4 hours before serving time, prepare Burnt Sugar Cake (page 111).

One and a half hours before serving time, prepare Baked Buttered Squash (page 110). One hour before serving, wash and dry leaves of 4 heads of Bibb lettuce and place in large salad bowl; chill. Just before serving, toss with ⅓ cup Italian-style salad dressing.

Twenty minutes before serving, cook 1 cup long-grain rice according to label directions; stir in ¼ cup chopped parsley. Fifteen minutes before serving, prepare Shrimp with Peppers (page 110) and serve with parslied rice.

SHRIMP WITH PEPPERS

½ cup butter or margarine
2 cups julienne strips green pepper
1 clove garlic, crushed
2 pounds shrimp, shelled and deveined
1½ cups dry white wine
½ teaspoon basil
¼ teaspoon thyme
1 bay leaf, crumbled
1 teaspoon salt
¼ teaspoon pepper
2 teaspoons cornstarch mixed with ¼ cup cold water (optional)

1. Melt butter or margarine in large heavy skillet over medium heat; add green pepper strips and garlic and sauté until green pepper is tender, about 5 minutes.

2. Add shrimp and cook just until pink. Stir in wine, basil, thyme and bay leaf. Simmer for 2 to 3 minutes. Add salt and pepper. If desired, thicken mixture with cornstarch stirred into water.

Note: This recipe can easily be doubled to serve eight.

BAKED BUTTERED SQUASH

4 medium-size acorn squash
1 cup water
½ cup butter or margarine
2 cups small whole mushrooms
2 tablespoons lemon juice
1 teaspoon grated lemon rind
¼ teaspoon salt
salt and pepper to taste

1. Cut squash lengthwise in half; scoop out and discard seeds and fibers. Place squash cut side down in well-greased 13 x 9 x 2-inch baking dish. Add water to dish and cover tightly with foil. Bake at 350° F for about 1 hour or until squash is just tender.

2. Meanwhile, melt ¼ cup of the butter or margarine in medium skillet over medium heat; add mushrooms and sauté until tender, about 5 to 7 minutes. Stir in lemon juice, lemon rind and ¼ teaspoon salt.

3. Turn squash over and season each cavity with 1 tablespoon of remaining butter or margarine and a little salt and pepper. Spoon one-fourth of mushroom mixture into each cavity. Bake 15 minutes longer, until squash is tender.

BURNT SUGAR CAKE

BURNT SUGAR SYRUP
1 cup sugar
1 cup boiling water

CAKE
½ cup butter or margarine
1½ cups sugar
3 eggs, separated
2¼ cups flour
2½ teaspoons baking
   powder
¼ teaspoon salt
1 cup evaporated milk
1 teaspoon vanilla extract
⅓ cup burnt sugar syrup
Burnt Sugar Frosting
   (below)
chopped pecans or toasted
   almonds (optional)

1. To make syrup, melt 1 cup sugar in large heavy skillet over low heat, stirring constantly. Remove from heat; gradually add boiling water, stirring constantly. Return to heat and bring to boiling point over high heat, stirring constantly. Reduce heat to low and cook for 2 to 3 minutes. Reserve ⅓ cup syrup for cake; set aside ⅔ cup to use for frosting.

2. Preheat oven to 350° F. Grease and flour two 9-inch cake pans.

3. To make cake, cream butter or margarine and 1½ cups sugar in large bowl until fluffy. Add egg yolks and beat until creamy and thick.

4. Mix flour, baking powder and salt. Add alternately with evaporated milk to creamed mixture. Beat until smooth. Stir in vanilla extract and reserved ⅓ cup syrup.

5. Turn batter into prepared cake pans. Bake for 25 to 30 minutes, until cake tester inserted in center comes out clean. Cool in pans on wire rack for 2 to 3 minutes, then turn out onto rack and cool completely. Fill and frost with Burnt Sugar Frosting; add chopped nuts to filling if desired. *Makes one 9-inch layer cake.*

Burnt Sugar Frosting

2 cups sugar
½ cup butter or margarine
1 cup evaporated milk
⅔ cup burnt sugar syrup
   (see cake recipe, above)
1 teaspoon vanilla extract

1. In large heavy saucepan, mix sugar, butter or margarine, evaporated milk and syrup. Bring to boiling point over medium heat, stirring constantly. Cook to soft ball stage (240° F on candy thermometer).

2. Remove from heat; stir in vanilla extract. Beat mixture until cool and thickened to spreading consistency (frosting will be like thick caramel). *Makes enough for one 9-inch layer cake.*

CASUAL BIRTHDAY PARTY

STEAK-BACON BURGERS*

OVEN FRIES AND DILLED PEAS*

HOT BUTTERED ITALIAN BREAD

TOSSED SALAD

CHOCOLATE* AND/OR FRESH APPLE* BIRTHDAY CAKE

ICE CREAM

COFFEE

For eight.

WORK PLAN: Several hours ahead of time, prepare Chocolate or Fresh Apple Birthday Cake (or prepare and serve both; see pages 113 and 114). Scoop 2 quarts coffee ice cream and place scoops on baking sheet; freeze. At dessert time, mound into bowl and serve with cake and coffee.

About 1½ hours before serving time, prepare Steak-Bacon Burgers through Step 2 (see recipe below); cover with plastic wrap and refrigerate until ready to cook. Prepare salad: Combine 4 cups tiny lettuce leaves and 2 cups each sliced tomatoes and cucumbers in large salad bowl; cover with plastic wrap and chill. Toss with 1 cup blue cheese dressing just before serving. Make Oven Fries and Dilled Peas (page 113). Cut 2 loaves Italian bread into ½-inch slices to within ¼ inch of bottom of loaves. Blend 1 cup butter or margarine, softened, and 2 cloves crushed garlic; spread garlic butter on both sides of each bread slice. Wrap loaves in foil; heat in oven while burgers are broiling.

STEAK-BACON BURGERS

2½ pounds ground sirloin
2 teaspoons salt
⅔ cup milk
½ cup unflavored yogurt or sour cream
2 tablespoons butter or margarine, softened
1 cup shredded sharp Cheddar cheese
2 tablespoons chopped onion or instant minced onion
8 slices bacon

1. Mix ground sirloin, salt and milk; shape into 8 patties. In small bowl, thoroughly mix yogurt or sour cream and butter or margarine; stir in cheese and onion.

2. Split each patty and place 1 tablespoon cheese filling on center of each bottom half. Replace top half of each and seal edges. Wrap 1 bacon slice around edge of each patty; secure with wooden toothpick.

3. Preheat broiler.

4. Arrange patties on rack in broiler pan. Broil 4 to 5 inches from heat for 8 to 10 minutes; turn patties and broil 5 minutes longer.

OVEN FRIES AND DILLED PEAS

8 medium potatoes
⅓ cup butter or margarine, melted
salt to taste
two 10-ounce packages frozen peas
3 tablespoons butter or margarine
1 teaspoon dried dill
¾ teaspoon salt
⅛ teaspoon pepper

1. Scrub and dry potatoes but do not peel. Cut lengthwise into eighths; arrange in 1 overlapping layer in greased 15 x 10 x 1-inch jelly-roll pan or large shallow baking pan.

2. Drizzle potatoes with ⅓ cup melted butter or margarine; sprinkle with salt to taste. Bake at 400° F for 40 to 45 minutes, stirring occasionally for more even browning.

3. When potatoes have been baking for about 20 minutes, place frozen peas in 2-quart casserole. Dot with 3 tablespoons butter or margarine; sprinkle with dill, ¾ teaspoon salt and the pepper. Cover casserole tightly and bake beside potatoes for 20 to 25 minutes.

CHOCOLATE BIRTHDAY CAKE

1 cup butter or margarine
2 cups sugar
2 teaspoons vanilla extract
½ cup unsweetened cocoa powder
4 eggs
2 cups flour
1 teaspoon baking soda
1 teaspoon salt
1 cup sour milk or buttermilk
Cocoa Frosting (below)

1. Preheat oven to 350° F. Grease and flour two 9-inch cake pans.

2. In large bowl, cream butter or margarine until softened. Add sugar gradually, creaming mixture until fluffy. Add vanilla extract and cocoa; blend well. Add eggs one at a time, beating well after each addition.

3. Sift flour, baking soda and salt onto waxed paper. Add dry ingredients alternately with milk to creamed mixture, beating well after each addition.

4. Divide batter between 2 prepared pans. Bake for 25 to 30 minutes, until cake tester inserted in center comes out clean. Cool in pans on wire rack for 8 minutes; remove from pans and cool completely on rack, then fill and frost with Cocoa Frosting. *Makes one 9-inch layer cake.*

Cocoa Frosting

⅓ cup butter or margarine, softened
⅓ cup unsweetened cocoa powder
1 egg
4 to 5 cups confectioners' sugar
⅓ cup milk, unflavored yogurt or sour cream
1 teaspoon vanilla extract
⅛ teaspoon salt

1. In medium bowl, cream butter or margarine with cocoa. Beat in egg.

2. Add confectioners' sugar alternately with milk, yogurt or sour cream, beating mixture until very smooth and of spreading consistency. Stir in vanilla extract and salt. *Makes enough for one 9-inch layer cake.*

FRESH APPLE BIRTHDAY CAKE

2½ cups sifted flour
1½ teaspoons baking soda
½ teaspoon salt
1 cup light brown sugar,
   firmly packed
1 cup granulated sugar
1 cup vegetable oil
3 eggs, slightly beaten
1 teaspoon vanilla extract
3 cups finely chopped,
   cored, peeled tart apples
Cream Cheese Frosting
   (below)
chopped nuts and raisins

1. Preheat oven to 350° F. Grease and flour two 9- or 10-inch cake pans, or grease one 10-inch tube pan. Sift flour, baking soda and salt onto waxed paper.

2. In large bowl, combine brown sugar and granulated sugar, oil and slightly beaten eggs. Beat until smooth. Add flour mixture, a scant cup at a time, beating well after each addition. Stir in vanilla extract; fold in apples.

3. Pour batter into prepared cake pan(s). Bake layers for 25 to 30 minutes, tube cake for 40 to 45 minutes. Cool in pan(s) on wire rack for 10 minutes, then turn out on rack to cool completely. Frost cake with Cream Cheese Frosting and decorate with nuts and raisins. *Makes one 9- or 10-inch layer cake or one 10-inch tube cake.*

Cream Cheese Frosting

one 8-ounce package cream
   cheese, softened
2 tablespoons butter or
   margarine
1 teaspoon vanilla extract
one 16-ounce package
   confectioners' sugar

1. In large bowl, mix cream cheese with butter or margarine. Stir in vanilla extract.

2. Sift in confectioners' sugar, about 1 cup at a time, beating until smooth. If necessary, beat in a little milk for better consistency. *Makes enough for one 9- or 10-inch layer cake or one 10-inch tube cake.*

SIXTEENTH BIRTHDAY PARTY

CREPES CORDON BLEU*

SPINACH-TOSS SALAD

RAINBOW CHIFFON
CAKE*

SODAS

For six to eight.

WORK PLAN: At least 4 hours before serving or a day ahead of time, prepare Rainbow Chiffon Cake (page 116). At the same time, make crepes for Crêpes Cordon Bleu (page 115).

One hour before serving time, combine 8 cups washed, torn spinach leaves with 1 cup crisply fried crumbled bacon and 1 cup seasoned croutons in very large salad bowl; cover and chill. Just before serving, toss with ¾ cup red wine vinegar and oil dressing.

Forty-five minutes before serving time, prepare filling and sauce for Crêpes Cordon Bleu, and bake crêpes as directed. *Pictured on page 103.*

CREPES CORDON BLEU

CREPES
1 cup flour
⅛ teaspoon salt
3 eggs
2 tablespoons vegetable oil
1½ cups milk

FILLING
2 cups diced cooked chicken
1 cup chopped cooked ham
1 cup shredded Swiss
   cheese
¼ teaspoon crumbled
   rosemary
milk or dry white wine

SAUCE
2 tablespoons butter or
   margarine
¼ cup chopped onion
one 10¾-ounce can
   condensed cream of
   mushroom soup
½ cup milk
½ cup dry white wine
1 cup sour cream

1 cup shredded Swiss
   cheese

1. To make crêpes, combine flour and salt in medium bowl. Using wire whisk, beat in eggs one at a time. Beat in oil. Gradually beat in 1½ cups milk. Continue beating until batter is very smooth and resembles light cream. Chill batter for about 2 hours.

2. To cook crêpes, grease 6-inch crêpe pan or small skillet and place over medium-high heat. Pour 2 to 3 tablespoons batter into hot pan; tip and swirl pan so batter covers bottom. After a few seconds, turn crêpe and lightly brown on second side.

3. Make 12 crêpes, greasing pan between each use. Crêpes can be made ahead, cooled and stacked with square of waxed paper between each. Overwrap and freeze until ready to use. Unwrap, separate and thaw while making filling and sauce.

4. To make filling, mix chicken, ham, 1 cup Swiss cheese and the rosemary in medium bowl. If mixture appears too dry, stir in 1 to 2 tablespoons milk or dry white wine. Set filling aside.

5. To make sauce, melt butter or margarine in medium saucepan over medium heat; add onion and sauté until tender, about 4 minutes. Mix in condensed soup. Blend in ½ cup milk and ½ cup dry white wine; raise heat to high and bring to boiling point. Remove from heat and fold in sour cream; set sauce aside.

6. To assemble crêpes, place about ⅓ cup filling in each; roll up jelly-roll fashion. Arrange filled crêpes in 2 greased 12 x 8 x 2-inch baking dishes. Spoon sauce over crêpes. Sprinkle with 1 cup Swiss cheese. Bake at 350° F for 35 minutes or until hot and bubbly.

RAINBOW CHIFFON CAKE

2 cups flour
1½ cups sugar
1 tablespoon baking powder
1 teaspoon salt
½ cup vegetable oil
7 eggs, separated
¾ cup water
1 teaspoon lemon extract or vanilla extract
½ teaspoon cream of tartar
2 tablespoons multicolored sprinkles
1 pint raspberry sherbet
1 pint orange sherbet
1 pint lime sherbet
1 pint heavy cream

1. Preheat oven to 325° F.

2. In large mixing bowl, stir together flour, sugar, baking powder and salt. Make a well in the center and add oil, egg yolks, water and extract. Beat well until very smooth.

3. Using electric mixer at high speed, beat egg whites and cream of tartar in large bowl until stiff. Using rubber spatula, fold whites into batter just until well blended. Fold in sprinkles.

4. Spoon batter into ungreased 10-inch tube pan. Bake for 60 to 65 minutes, until top springs back when lightly touched. Invert pan and cool cake for 45 minutes; loosen and turn out on wire rack to cool completely.

5. Cut 1-inch slice from top of cooled cake and set slice aside. Hollow out a ring in cake, leaving 1-inch-thick shell.

6. Fill hollow with alternating tiny scoops of raspberry, orange and lime sherbets. Replace top slice and freeze cake until filling is firm, about 2 hours.

7. Stiffly beat cream; use to frost cake, making rosettes or swirls on top for candles. (Whipped cream frosting may be tinted if desired.) Freeze again until firm, about 45 to 60 minutes. *Makes one 10-inch tube cake.*

Note: A store-bought 10-inch tube sponge cake may be substituted for the homemade cake.

An ice cream- or sherbet-filled cake provides the perfect party climax after "Happy Birthday" has been sung, the wish has been made and the candles blown out. For this kind of cake, it's important to work quickly, both when you're making it and when you're serving it. Return it to the freezer immediately after doling out dessert portions so the cake doesn't get soggy with melted filling. If properly wrapped, these cakes keep up to two months, but they're such favorites you won't have leftovers for long!

BIRTHDAY PARTY FOR KIDS

CRISPY DRUMSTICKS*

LITTLE BUTTERED ROLLS

CARROT AND CELERY STICKS

SUSANNAH'S ZINGIE CAKE*

ICE CREAM

LEMONADE   MILK

For eight.

WORK PLAN: At least 4 hours before serving time, prepare Susannah's Zingie Cake (page 118).

One hour before serving time, prepare Crispy Drumsticks (below).

Twenty minutes ahead of time, bake two 8-ounce packages refrigerator buttermilk biscuits according to label directions; split, butter and serve hot along with chicken. At the same time, prepare 2 cups each celery and carrot sticks, and serve with chicken.

At dessert time, scoop 2 quarts strawberry ice cream into 8 dessert dishes and serve with or after the birthday cake. (Or do this ahead while making the cake and store individual desserts in freezer until serving time.)

Serve kids a choice of lemonade or milk.

CRISPY DRUMSTICKS

8 chicken legs with thighs
¼ cup butter or margarine, melted
1 cup finely crushed potato chips

1. Preheat oven to 375° F.

2. Brush chicken legs with melted butter or margarine. Roll in crushed potato chips until completely coated.

3. Arrange prepared chicken legs in shallow baking pan or jelly-roll pan. Bake for 40 to 45 minutes, until meat is fork-tender.

SUSANNAH'S ZINGIE CAKE

½ cup butter or margarine
2¼ cups flour
1½ cups sugar
3 teaspoons baking powder
1 teaspoon salt
1 cup milk
2 eggs
1 teaspoon vanilla extract
one 3-ounce package red
   raspberry-flavored gelatin
Zingie Frosting (below)
pastel candy sticks
prepared frosting gel in tube

1. Preheat oven to 350° F. Grease and flour two 8- or 9-inch cake pans.

2. Using electric mixer at medium speed, beat butter or margarine in large bowl until creamy. In medium bowl, stir together flour, sugar, baking powder and salt.

3. Blend dry ingredients into butter or margarine; blend in ⅔ cup of the milk. Mix for 2 minutes at medium speed. Add remaining ⅓ cup milk, the eggs and vanilla extract; beat 2 minutes longer. Divide half the batter between 2 prepared pans.

4. Add 3 tablespoons of the gelatin powder to batter remaining in bowl; mix well. (Reserve remaining gelatin powder for frosting.) Drop spoonfuls of colored batter on top of white batter. Zigzag a spoon or small spatula through batter to marbleize.

5. Bake for 25 to 30 minutes, until cake springs back when lightly touched. Cool for 5 minutes in pans on wire rack, then turn out on rack and cool completely. Fill and frost cooled cake with Zingie Frosting. Decorate with upright pastel candy sticks around sides; write name of the birthday child on top of the cake with prepared frosting gel. *Makes one 8- or 9-inch layer cake.*

Zingie Frosting

⅓ cup butter or margarine
2½ tablespoons red
   raspberry gelatin powder
   (remaining from cake
   recipe, above)
3 to 3½ cups confectioners'
   sugar
3 to 4 tablespoons milk
1 teaspoon vanilla extract

1. Using electric mixer at medium speed, cream butter or margarine with gelatin powder in small bowl.

2. Add confectioners' sugar alternately with milk until mixture is of spreading consistency. Stir in vanilla extract. *Makes enough for one 8- or 9-inch layer cake.*

Desserts and Drinks

W*hat better way to stretch out a pleasant day or evening than with drinks or coffee and dessert? And what an ideal way to extend your hospitality to lots of people—one-course entertaining!*

Invite people over to cool off on a hot summer evening with a duo of fresh fruit desserts—Peaches Cardinal and Pears with Sabayon Sauce—served with a pitcher of icy Sangria. When the weather turns cold, a festive Pumpkin Chiffon Pie or Nutmeg Cake with Hot Buttered Rum will provide instant holiday cheer. Whatever the season, a soufflé or mousse accompanied by Café Brûlot or Café de Minta could give dessert a whole new meaning.

Keep these tips in mind for an outstanding drinks-and-dessert party.

- *For best results, refrigerate do-aheads rather than freezing them.*
- *Add garnishes at the last minute for show-stopping desserts.*
- *Set these recipes off with your most attractive dishes.*
- *Stick to the ingredients given in the drink recipes to preserve the flavor balance. Remember: 2 ounces is 1/4 cup; 1 ounce equals 2 tablespoons; a shot glass is usually 1 1/2 ounces.*
- *With liqueurs, 1 quart will serve 16 people generously; a fifth is fine for 12 guests.*
- *Add soda water, sparkling wines and ice to punch just before serving.*
- *Freshly brewed coffee is imperative! And freshly ground coffee can be the crowning glory of a meal.*

Follow these tips along with the recipes in this chapter and you'll convince all comers that as far as courses are concerned, last is best!

FRENCH APPLE TART

PASTRY CRUST
1 cup flour
½ cup butter or margarine, softened
1 egg yolk
2 tablespoons sugar
1 teaspoon finely grated lemon rind

FILLING
3 pounds tart apples, peeled, quartered and cored
⅓ cup golden raisins
¼ cup sugar
¼ cup lemon juice
3 tablespoons water
½ cup finely chopped almonds

TOPPING
1 pound tart apples
1 egg white
1 tablespoon lemon juice

GLAZE
½ cup apricot preserves, strained
2 tablespoons sugar

1. To make pastry crust, place flour, butter or margarine, egg yolk, 2 tablespoons sugar and the lemon rind in food processor bowl; process until mixture leaves side of bowl clean and forms a smooth ball. (Or mix in small bowl and knead by hand.) Wrap in waxed paper and refrigerate for 30 minutes.

2. Grease and flour 9-inch pie plate. Roll out dough to 11-inch circle on lightly floured pastry cloth or board; fit into pie plate. Refrigerate while making filling.

3. To make filling, combine 3 pounds apples, the raisins, ¼ cup sugar, ¼ cup lemon juice and the water in large saucepan. Bring to boiling point over medium heat. Reduce heat to low and simmer for 10 minutes. Stir in almonds. Cool.

4. Preheat oven to 300° F.

5. Spoon cooled apple filling into pie shell. To make topping, peel, core and thinly slice 1 pound apples. Arrange in 2 overlapping concentric circles over filling. Brush with egg white and sprinkle with 1 tablespoon lemon juice.

6. Bake for 1 hour or until crust is deep golden brown and top apple slices are tender. Cool slightly on wire rack.

7. To make glaze, melt apricot preserves with 2 tablespoons sugar in small saucepan over low heat. Brush onto warm tart. *Serves eight. Pictured on page 104.*

Note: This tart may be made ahead of time, then frozen for up to 3 months. When cool, stick toothpicks into top of tart before covering completely with plastic wrap. (Toothpicks prevent plastic wrap from spoiling glaze.) To thaw, let stand at room temperature for 1 hour; remove plastic wrap and toothpicks before serving.

Preheat oven to 400° F.

. To make crust, combine crumbs, chopped pecans, ½ cup melted butter or margarine and granulated sugar n medium bowl until well blended. Press into 11-inch juiche pan. Bake for 5 minutes; cool crust completely on wire rack.

3. To make filling, use electric mixer at high speed to cream 1 cup softened butter or margarine and the confectioners' sugar in medium bowl until light and fluffy. Add eggs one at a time, beating well after each addition. Add rum, bourbon and brandy, 1 tablespoon at a time, beating after each addition.

4. Pile mixture into cooled crust. Refrigerate overnight. At serving time, garnish with large pecan halves, chopped pecans and whole strawberries if desired. *Serves ten.*

Note: Eggnog Pie may be frozen for up to 3 months. After piling filling into crust, freeze pie uncovered until solid, then wrap in aluminum foil. Thaw in refrigerator for several hours or overnight before serving.

1 cup butter or margarine, softened
one 16-ounce package confectioners' sugar
5 eggs
3 tablespoons light rum
3 tablespoons bourbon
1 tablespoon brandy
pecan halves, chopped pecans, whole strawberries (optional)

GRASSHOPPER PIE

CRUST
1½ cups chocolate wafer crumbs
¼ cup sugar
¼ cup butter or margarine, melted

FILLING
1 envelope unflavored gelatin
1⅓ cups heavy cream
4 egg yolks
¼ cup sugar
¼ cup white crème de cacao
¼ cup green crème de menthe
chocolate curls

1. Preheat oven to 350° F.

2. To make crust, combine chocolate crumbs, ¼ cup sugar and melted butter or margarine in medium bowl until well blended. Press into 9-inch pie plate. Bake for 5 minutes, until crust is set. Cool completely on wire rack.

3. To make filling, sprinkle gelatin over ⅓ cup of the cream in small heavy saucepan. Heat over very low heat, stirring constantly, until gelatin is dissolved.

4. Using electric mixer at high speed, beat egg yolks in medium bowl until thick and lemon colored. Gradually beat in ¼ cup sugar. Stir in crème de cacao and crème de menthe, then gelatin mixture. Refrigerate until mixture is consistency of unbeaten egg whites, about 45 minutes.

5. Using electric mixer at high speed, beat remaining 1 cup cream in another medium bowl until stiff. Fold into syrupy gelatin mixture. Pour mixture into pie shell. Refrigerate for 5 hours or until filling is firm. Garnish with chocolate curls. *Serves six to eight.*

SNAPPY LEMON DESSERT

CRUST
2 cups crushed gingersnaps
½ cup sugar
⅔ cup butter or margarine,
melted

FILLING
6 eggs
1½ cups sugar
½ cup lemon juice
2 teaspoons finely grated
lemon rind
½ cup butter or margarine

TOPPING
1½ cups heavy cream
2 tablespoons sugar
1 teaspoon vanilla extract

1. To make crust, combine gingersnap crumbs, ½ cup sugar and ⅔ cup melted butter or margarine in small bowl. Firmly pat mixture into greased 10-inch springform pan, pressing up side of pan to height of 1½ inches. Refrigerate for 30 minutes.

2. Preheat oven to 375° F.

3. Meanwhile, make filling by using electric mixer at high speed to beat eggs in medium bowl. Add 1½ cups sugar and beat until thick and lemon colored. Add lemon juice and rind. Slowly pour filling into chilled crust. Slice ½ cup butter or margarine and place pats on top of filling.

4. Bake for 25 minutes or until medium brown. Filling will firm up as it cools. Cool completely in pan on wire rack. Cut off crust that extends above filling, sprinkling crumbs on top as they fall. Refrigerate for at least 1 hour.

5. To make topping, use electric mixer at high speed to beat cream, 2 tablespoons sugar and the vanilla extract in small bowl until stiff. Remove side of pan. Spread beaten cream on top of dessert, swirling with back of teaspoon. *Serves ten.*

MARBLE RUM PIE

1 envelope unflavored
gelatin
1 cup sugar
⅛ teaspoon salt
1 cup milk
2 eggs, separated
one 12-ounce package
semisweet chocolate
morsels
¼ cup dark rum
1 cup heavy cream
1 teaspoon vanilla extract
one baked 9-inch pie shell
(see recipe for Great
Piecrust, page 105)

1. In top of double boiler, mix gelatin, ¼ cup of the sugar and the salt. Beat in milk and egg yolks. Place over hot (not boiling) water; stir constantly until mixture thickens. Add chocolate; stir until melted. Remove from heat.

2. Stir in rum. Refrigerate until mixture is consistency of unbeaten egg whites, about 45 minutes.

3. Using electric mixer at high speed, beat egg whites in small bowl until foamy-white and doubled in volume. Gradually beat in ½ cup of the remaining sugar, 1 tablespoon at a time; continue beating until meringue is glossy and forms stiff peaks. Fold into chocolate mixture.

4. In another small bowl, use mixer at high speed to beat cream with remaining ¼ cup sugar and the vanilla extract until stiff.

5. Alternate large mounds of chocolate and vanilla mixtures to fill pie shell. Swirl with a spoon to marbleize. Chill until serving time. *Serves eight.*

PEAR-ALMOND TART

PASTRY CRUST
1 cup butter or margarine, softened
two 3-ounce packages cream cheese, softened
2 cups flour
¼ teaspoon salt

CREME PATISSERIE
6 egg yolks
½ cup sugar
½ cup flour
2 cups milk
3 tablespoons butter or margarine
2 tablespoons anise liqueur
1 tablespoons vanilla extract

Poached Pears (below)
1 cup apricot preserves, strained
30 whole unblanched almonds

1. To make pastry crust, combine 1 cup butter or margarine and the cream cheese in medium bowl. Work in 2 cups flour and the salt until mixture forms a ball. Wrap in waxed paper and refrigerate for 1 hour.

2. Roll out pastry to 14-inch circle on lightly floured pastry cloth or board. Line 12-inch flan or pie pan with pastry. Prick all over bottom and refrigerate for 30 minutes.

3. Preheat oven to 450° F.

4. Bake crust for 5 to 7 minutes, until it begins to brown. Open oven and burst pastry bubbles with fork. Reduce heat to 400° F and bake 5 minutes longer, until rich golden brown. Cool completely in pan on wire rack.

5. To make crème patisserie, use electric mixer at high speed to beat egg yolks in heavy saucepan. Gradually add sugar, beating until mixture is thick and lemon colored. Beat in ½ cup flour.

6. Scald milk in medium saucepan; slowly add to yolk mixture. Place over low heat. Heat for about 2 minutes, stirring constantly with wire whisk to remove lumps and keep mixture smooth, until mixture is consistency of mayonnaise. Remove from heat and beat in 3 tablespoons butter or margarine, the liqueur and vanilla extract. Cover surface with waxed paper and refrigerate.

7. Make Poached Pears. Melt strained preserves in small saucepan over low heat, adding a little water, if necessary, to make a spreadable glaze. Brush bottom of tart shell with a little glaze; reserve remaining glaze.

8. To assemble tart, pour chilled crème patisserie into glazed tart shell shortly before serving. Arrange Poached Pears in spoke fashion on top, stem ends in, leaving center free. Arrange almonds between pear halves and in a star in center. Reheat reserved glaze and brush over entire top surface of tart. *Serves ten to twelve.*

Poached Pears

3 large firm pears
4 cups cold water
1 tablespoon lemon juice
4 cups water
½ cup sugar

1. Peel, core and halve pears. Drop into bowl with 4 cups cold water and the lemon juice.

2. Bring 4 cups water and the sugar to boiling point in large saucepan. Drain pears and add to syrup. Reduce heat to low and simmer for 10 minutes or until tender. Cool pears; drain from syrup and chill. *Makes 3.*

PUMPKIN CHIFFON PIE

Nut Crust (below)
¾ cup brown sugar, firmly
   packed
1 envelope unflavored
   gelatin
2 teaspoons cinnamon
½ teaspoon ginger
½ teaspoon allspice
½ teaspoon salt
½ cup milk
½ cup cold water
3 eggs, separated
one 16-ounce can pumpkin
¼ teaspoon cream of tartar
⅓ cup granulated sugar
1 cup heavy cream
pecan halves

1. Prepare Nut Crust and cool as directed.

2. In top of double boiler, combine brown sugar, gelatin, cinnamon, ginger, allspice and salt. In small bowl, beat milk, cold water and egg yolks until well mixed. Stir into gelatin mixture. Stir in pumpkin. Cook over boiling water, stirring often, for 20 minutes or until mixture thickens. Refrigerate until cool and syrupy, about 30 minutes.

3. Using electric mixer at high speed, beat egg whites with cream of tartar in small deep bowl until soft peaks form. Add granulated sugar, 1 tablespoon at a time, beating well after each addition; beat until mixture forms stiff peaks.

4. Without washing beaters, beat syrupy pumpkin mixture until foamy and doubled in volume. Fold in beaten egg whites. Spoon into cooled Nut Crust. Refrigerate for at least 2 hours.

5. At serving time, beat cream until stiff; spread over pie. Garnish with pecan halves. *Serves eight.*

Nut Crust

1⅜ cups flour
¼ cup finely chopped pecans
   or walnuts
1 teaspoon salt
⅜ cup vegetable oil
3 tablespoons cold milk

1. Preheat oven to 450° F.

2. In small bowl, mix flour and nuts. Make a well in the center.

3. In 1-cup measure, mix oil and milk. Pour into dry ingredients. Mix together until dough leaves side of bowl and forms a ball.

4. Roll out between two sheets of waxed paper to form 12-inch circle; fit into 9-inch pie plate. Prick with fork. Bake for 12 to 15 minutes, until golden. Cool completely on wire rack. *Makes one 9-inch crust.*

PROFITEROLES WITH CHOCOLATE-HONEY SAUCE

1 cup water
⅜ cup butter or margarine
1 teaspoon sugar
⅛ teaspoon salt
1 cup flour
5 eggs
½ teaspoon water
1 quart butter almond ice cream, or 2 cups heavy cream, stiffly beaten
Chocolate-Honey Sauce (below)
one 2½-ounce package sliced almonds (optional)

1. Preheat oven to 400° F.

2. In heavy saucepan, combine 1 cup water, the butter or margarine, sugar and salt. Bring to boiling point over medium heat to melt butter or margarine. Remove from heat.

3. Beat in flour all at once. Return pan to heat and cook, stirring, until mixture forms a ball and begins to film bottom of pan. Remove from heat. Beat in 4 eggs one at a time, beating very well after each addition.

4. Make 1¼-inch-wide mounds, 2 inches apart, on 2 greased baking sheets. Slightly beat remaining egg with ½ teaspoon water; brush on top of each puff, being careful not to get any egg on baking sheets.

5. Place one sheet in upper third of oven, the other in lower third. Bake for 15 to 20 minutes or until puffs are doubled in size and lightly browned. Remove from oven, make a small slit in each puff with a knife and return to oven. Turn off heat. Leave door ajar and let puffs remain in oven for 10 minutes. Cool on sheets on wire racks. (If not to be eaten within a day, store in airtight containers or plastic bags. Keep at room temperature or freeze. Refresh in 400° F oven for 2 to 3 minutes.)

6. At serving time, split puffs in half. Fill with ice cream or stiffly beaten heavy cream. Place filled puffs in glass serving bowls. Pour Chocolate-Honey Sauce over each portion. Top with sliced almonds if desired. *Serves eight.*

Chocolate-Honey Sauce

one 12-ounce package semisweet chocolate morsels
¼ cup heavy cream
2 tablespoons honey
1 teaspoon vanilla extract
⅛ teaspoon salt

1. Place chocolate in top of double boiler over hot water to melt. Remove from heat.

2. Stir in cream, honey, vanilla extract and salt; beat until creamy. Serve warm. *Makes 1 cup.*

NEVER-FAIL ANGEL FOOD-BRICKLE CAKE

ANGEL FOOD CAKE
1½ cups sifted
  confectioners' sugar
1 cup flour
1½ cups egg whites (about
  12)
1½ teaspoons cream of
  tartar
¼ teaspoon salt
1 cup granulated sugar
1½ teaspoons vanilla extract
½ teaspoon almond extract

FILLING AND FROSTING
2½ cups heavy cream
1 teaspoon vanilla extract
one 10-ounce jar
  butterscotch sauce
half of 7.8-ounce package
  brickle

1. Preheat oven to 375° F.

2. To make angel food cake, sift confectioners' sugar and flour together onto waxed paper; set aside.

3. In large bowl, beat egg whites, cream of tartar and salt until soft peaks form. Add granulated sugar, 1 tablespoon at a time, beating well after each addition, until stiff peaks form. Fold in flour mixture, then 1½ teaspoons vanilla extract and the almond extract. Spoon into ungreased 11-inch tube pan.

4. Bake for 30 to 35 minutes, until cake springs back when lightly touched. Invert pan onto funnel or bottle and let cool completely; remove from pan. With long sharp knife, split cooled cake into 3 layers.

5. To make filling and frosting, beat cream in medium bowl until stiff. Add 1 teaspoon vanilla extract. Fold in butterscotch sauce. Grind brickle in blender or food processor until very fine.

6. Place 1 cake layer on serving plate. Spread with some of cream mixture and sprinkle with half of brickle. Repeat. Add third cake layer and frost top and sides. Refrigerate for at least 6 hours. *Serves ten.*

Note: If desired, this cake can be made ahead of time and frozen for up to 4 weeks. Stick toothpicks at 3-inch intervals into top and sides of cake; cover completely with plastic wrap. (Toothpicks prevent plastic wrap from touching frosting.) To thaw, place in refrigerator for 5 to 6 hours; remove plastic wrap and toothpicks before serving cake.

If your shopping forays haven't turned up any brickle, buy some peanut brittle as a substitute. Just grind it in a blender or food processor as directed for the brickle in the fifth step of the recipe above, or crush it between sheets of waxed paper with a rolling pin. Peanut brittle will, of course, give a different flavor from brickle, which tastes like toffee.

CHRISTMAS ANGEL-RUM CAKE

2½ cups milk
½ cup sugar
¼ cup cornstarch
2 eggs
½ teaspoon salt
1 teaspoon vanilla extract
1 teaspoon almond extract
red food coloring
green food coloring
half of one 1-ounce square
  unsweetened chocolate,
  melted and cooled
one 9- or 10-inch angel food
  cake
¼ cup rum
¼ cup sherry
½ cup heavy cream
1 tablespoon sugar
chocolate curls from one
  1-ounce square semisweet
  chocolate

1. In top of double boiler, combine milk, ½ cup sugar, the cornstarch, eggs and salt. Cook over boiling water, stirring frequently, until thickened, about 10 minutes. Remove from water and cool. Add vanilla extract and almond extract; stir to blend well.

2. Divide custard among 3 small bowls. Using food coloring, color one part pink and one part green. Color remaining part brown with melted chocolate.

3. Cut cake into 4 layers, each about 1 inch thick (use toothpicks to mark cake into layers before cutting). In small bowl, combine rum and sherry.

4. To assemble cake, place bottom layer on serving plate; sprinkle with one-fourth of liquor and 1 part of custard. Repeat twice. Top with remaining cake layer and sprinkle with remaining liquor. Refrigerate for several hours or overnight.

5. At serving time, beat cream with 1 tablespoon sugar until stiff. Top cake with beaten cream. Decorate with chocolate curls. *Serves twelve.*

APRICOT BRANDY POUND CAKE

3 cups flour
½ teaspoon salt
¼ teaspoon baking soda
1 cup butter or margarine,
  softened
3 cups granulated sugar
6 eggs
1 cup sour cream
½ cup apricot brandy
1 tablespoon orange liqueur
1 teaspoon vanilla extract
¼ teaspoon almond extract
confectioners' sugar

1. Preheat oven to 350° F. Grease and flour 10-inch tube pan. Sift flour, salt and baking soda onto waxed paper.

2. Using electric mixer at high speed, cream butter or margarine and granulated sugar in large bowl until light and fluffy. Add eggs one at a time, beating well after each addition.

3. In small bowl, mix sour cream, apricot brandy, orange liqueur, vanilla extract and almond extract until well blended. Add to creamed butter mixture alternately with sifted dry ingredients, beginning and ending with the dry ingredients.

4. Spoon batter into prepared pan. Bake for 1 hour or until cake tester inserted in center comes out clean. Let cake cool in pan on wire rack for 30 minutes. Loosen cake around edge and tube with long sharp knife. Invert onto rack; cool completely. Just before serving, sift confectioners' sugar over top of cake. *Serves ten to twelve.*

CHOCOLATE-CHESTNUT LOAF

12 ladyfingers, split
¼ cup brandy
two 1-ounce squares
  unsweetened chocolate
3 tablespoons butter or
  margarine
2 tablespoons water
one 15½-ounce can chestnut
  puree
¾ cup sugar
1 cup heavy cream

1. Butter 9 x 5 x 3-inch loaf pan. Line bottom and sides with split ladyfingers. Sprinkle ladyfingers with 2 tablespoons of the brandy.

2. In top of double boiler over hot (not boiling) water, heat chocolate, butter or margarine and water, stirring often, until chocolate melts and mixture is smooth.

3. Beat in chestnut puree, sugar and remaining 2 tablespoons brandy until well blended. Pour into ladyfinger-lined pan. Refrigerate for at least 3 hours or overnight.

4. At serving time, run a small sharp knife around edges of pan. Invert onto serving platter. Stiffly beat heavy cream and spread over loaf. *Serves eight.*

CHOCOLATE MOCHA CAKE

two 15.5-ounce boxes
  double fudge brownie mix
one 6-ounce package
  semisweet chocolate
  morsels, melted and
  cooled
3 eggs
½ cup water
1 tablespoon instant
  espresso coffee powder
Mocha Frosting (below)

1. Preheat oven to 350° F. Grease two 9-inch cake pans. Line bottoms with waxed paper circles; grease paper. Remove flavor packets from brownie mixes, reserving 1 packet for Mocha Frosting.

2. In large bowl, combine brownie mix, melted chocolate, eggs, water and coffee powder. Beat until well blended, 50 strokes with wooden spoon or 30 seconds with electric mixer at high speed. Pour into prepared pans.

3. Bake for 30 minutes or until cake tester inserted in center comes out clean. Cool in pans on wire rack for 10 minutes. Invert onto wire rack and peel off paper. Flip cakes top side up; cool completely on rack. Fill and frost with Mocha Frosting. *Serves eight to ten.*

Note: Cake can be refrigerated or frozen. If frozen, cover with plastic wrap or aluminum foil only after cake is firm. Freeze for up to 4 weeks; unwrap before thawing.

Mocha Frosting

3 cups confectioners' sugar
2 teaspoons instant
  espresso coffee powder
1 brownie mix flavor packet
  (from cake recipe, above)
¾ cup heavy cream
1 tablespoon butter or
  margarine, melted
¼ cup chopped walnuts

1. Sift confectioners' sugar and coffee powder into large bowl.

2. Add brownie flavor packet, cream, melted butter or margarine and walnuts. Stir to blend well. *Makes enough for one 9-inch layer cake.*

NUTMEG CAKE

3 cups flour
2 teaspoons nutmeg
1 teaspoon baking powder
1 teaspoon baking soda
¼ teaspoon salt
½ cup butter or margarine
1½ cups granulated sugar
3 eggs
1 teaspoon vanilla extract
1 cup buttermilk

PECAN-COCONUT TOPPING
½ cup butter or margarine,
melted
1 cup brown sugar, firmly
packed
1 teaspoon vanilla extract
1 cup flaked coconut
1 cup chopped pecans

stiffly beaten heavy cream
(optional)

1. Preheat oven to 350° F. Grease and flour 13 x 9 x 2-inch baking pan. Sift flour, nutmeg, baking powder, baking soda and salt onto waxed paper.

2. In large bowl, cream ½ cup butter or margarine and the granulated sugar until light and fluffy. Add eggs one at a time, beating well after each addition. Add 1 teaspoon vanilla extract. Add dry ingredients alternately with buttermilk, beginning and ending with dry ingredients. Pour batter into prepared pan.

3. Bake for about 35 minutes, until center springs back when lightly touched. Let cool in pan on wire rack for 15 minutes. Raise oven temperature to broil.

4. To make pecan-coconut topping, combine ½ cup melted butter or margarine, the brown sugar, 1 teaspoon vanilla extract, the coconut and pecans in medium bowl; spread over slightly cooled cake. Broil for 2 minutes or until topping bubbles and browns; do not overcook. Cool in pan on wire rack. Cut into squares and serve with stiffly beaten cream if desired. *Serves eight to twelve.*

Note: One cup sweet milk mixed with 2 tablespoons vinegar may be substituted for the buttermilk in this recipe.

A moist, rich confection like this Nutmeg Cake deserves the best ingredients—including freshly ground nutmeg. If you're fond of baking cakes, pies, cookies and sweet breads, it's worth your while to invest in some whole nutmeg cloves and a small nutmeg grater. Not ony will you be sure your nutmeg is strictly fresh and will impart its optimum flavor, but the incomparable fragrance of the freshly ground spice wafting through your kitchen will make any baking day seem special. Be sure to store nutmeg cloves in an airtight container.

RIGO JANCSE

CAKE
three 1-ounce squares
  unsweetened chocolate
¾ cup butter or margarine,
  softened
½ cup sugar
4 eggs, separated
⅛ teaspoon salt
½ cup sifted flour

FILLING
1½ cups heavy cream
10 ounces semisweet
  chocolate, broken (from
  one 16-ounce block)
¼ cup dark rum
1 teaspoon vanilla extract

GLAZE
1 cup sugar
⅓ cup water
6 ounces semisweet
  chocolate (remaining
  from one 16-ounce block)

1. Preheat oven to 350° F. Grease and flour 15 x 10 x 1-inch jelly-roll pan.

2. To make cake, melt unsweetened chocolate in small saucepan over low heat; cool. Cream butter or margarine with ¼ cup of the sugar until light and fluffy. Mix chocolate into creamed mixture. Beat in egg yolks one at a time.

3. Using electric mixer at high speed, beat egg whites and salt in large bowl until frothy. Gradually add remaining ¼ cup sugar, beating until mixture forms stiff meringue. Fold meringue mixture into chocolate mixture.

4. Sprinkle flour over surface of mixture; fold in gently until all flour disappears. Turn batter into prepared pan and spread evenly.

5. Bake for 15 to 18 minutes, until cake tester inserted in center comes out clean. Cool in pan on wire rack for 10 minutes. Remove from pan to rack to cool completely.

6. Meanwhile, make filling by combining cream and 10 ounces semisweet chocolate in medium saucepan; stir over medium heat until smooth. Reduce heat to low; continue to stir until mixture thickens. Pour into bowl; refrigerate for 1 hour. Add rum and vanilla extract; beat until very smooth, creamy and thick.

7. Cut cooled cake in half, making 2 rectangles about 5 x 7 inches. Spread filling on 1 layer; top with second layer and chill for 1 hour.

8. To make glaze, mix 1 cup sugar, the water and 6 ounces semisweet chocolate in medium saucepan over medium heat; stir until chocolate melts. Remove pan from heat and cool for 20 minutes. Place chilled cake on wire rack over foil; pour glaze over cake. Chill 30 minutes longer, until glaze is set and cold. *Serves eight to ten.*

Note: This cake is named for a famous Hungarian folk hero, Rigo Jancse (not, as is popularly thought, for the town of Riga in Latvia).

WHIPPED CREAM CAKE

CAKE
1½ cups flour
2 teaspoons baking powder
3 eggs
1½ cups granulated sugar
2 teaspoons vanilla extract
1½ cups heavy cream
1 cup finely ground
   packaged brickle or
   peanut brittle

CHOCOLATE BUTTERCREAM
one 1-ounce square
   semisweet chocolate
3 tablespoons butter or
   margarine
1 egg yolk
⅓ cup sifted confectioners'
   sugar

WHIPPED TOPPING
1 cup heavy cream
1 tablespoon granulated
   sugar
1 teaspoon vanilla extract

1. Preheat oven to 350° F. Grease two 9-inch cake pans. Line bottoms with waxed paper circles; grease paper.

2. To make cake, sift flour and baking powder onto sheet of waxed paper; set aside.

3. Using electric mixer at high speed, beat eggs in large bowl. Gradually add 1½ cups granulated sugar, beating until mixture is thick and lemon colored. With mixer at low speed, blend in 2 teaspoons vanilla extract. Fold in sifted dry ingredients.

4. In medium bowl, beat 1½ cups cream until stiff. Fold into batter, then fold in ground brickle or peanut brittle. Pour batter into prepared pans.

5. Bake for 25 minutes or until cake just begins to pull away from sides of pans. Cool in pans on wire rack for 10 minutes. Invert onto rack and immediately remove waxed paper. Flip layers top side up; cool completely.

6. To make chocolate buttercream, melt chocolate and butter or margarine in small saucepan; cool slightly. In small bowl, combine egg yolk, confectioners' sugar and melted chocolate mixture. Using electric mixer at medium speed, beat until very smooth and creamy; set aside.

7. To make whipped topping, beat 1 cup cream in small deep bowl until almost stiff. Add 1 tablespoon granulated sugar and 1 teaspoon vanilla extract. Continue beating just until stiff.

8. To assemble cake, sandwich layers with chocolate buttercream. Frost top and sides with whipped topping. *Serves ten to twelve.*

Whipped cream toppings and frostings are the crowning touch on extravagantly rich desserts like this Whipped Cream Cake. Chill the bowl and beaters in the refrigerator before beating the heavy cream. Buy the freshest cream you can find (avoid pasteurized cream, if possible) and don't overbeat—you could end up with butter! When flavoring cream do not over-measure extracts, liqueurs or fruit juices; too much will make the whipped cream lose its stiffness. Follow these tips and you'll achieve the peak of success every time.

ALMOND TORTE

1½ cups blanched almonds
2 tablespoons butter or margarine, softened
2 tablespoons fine bread crumbs
2 whole eggs
6 egg yolks
½ cup sugar
⅓ cup flour
8 egg whites

RUM GLAZE
2¼ cups confectioners' sugar
2 tablespoons light rum
1 egg white
1 tablespoon lemon juice

½ cup raspberry jam

1. Preheat oven to 350° F.

2. Spread almonds on cookie sheet. Toast in preheating oven for 5 to 10 minutes, until golden brown. In electric blender, pulverize a handful at a time to a fine powder; set aside. Use softened butter or margarine to grease sides and bottoms of two 9-inch cake pans; dust with bread crumbs.

3. Using electric mixer at high speed, beat whole eggs and 6 yolks in large bowl until thick and lemon colored. Gradually add sugar and beat until a ribbon forms when beaters are lifted. Beat in flour and ground almonds. Wash beaters very well.

4. Using electric mixer at high speed, beat egg whites in another large bowl until stiff. Very gently fold into almond mixture. Spread evenly in prepared pans.

5. Bake for 20 minutes or until toothpick inserted in center comes out clean. Cool in pans on wire rack for 5 minutes. Gently loosen around edge of pans with long sharp knife. Invert onto wire rack; cool completely.

6. To make rum glaze, beat together confectioners' sugar, rum, egg white and lemon juice in small bowl until very smooth; if too thin, add more confectioners' sugar.

7. To assemble cake, spread jam between 2 cooled layers. Pour glaze over top of cake, smoothing it and letting it drizzle over side. *Serves ten to twelve.*

If you're thinking of having people over for dessert and coffee and can't decide what to serve from your usual pie-and-cake repertoire, try making a torte, which is a favorite throughout Europe; it's a lighter, yet richer, substitute for cake. The Almond Torte, above, as well as the other tortes in this section will win you raves on the party-going scene.

CHOCOLATE TORTE

1½ cups egg whites (about 12 medium)
2½ cups superfine sugar
1 teaspoon baking powder
¼ teaspoon salt
1 tablespoon white vinegar
2 teaspoons vanilla extract
1 cup heavy cream
1 tablespoon superfine sugar
Buttercream Filling (below)
half of store-bought 9-inch angel food cake
1 cup ground pecans

1. Preheat oven to 300° F.

2. Using electric mixer at high speed, beat egg whites in large bowl until foamy-white and doubled in volume. In small bowl, combine 2½ cups superfine sugar, the baking powder and salt; sprinkle over surface of egg whites, ¼ cup at a time, beating well after each addition. Beat until meringue is glossy and stiff peaks form. Beat in vinegar and 1 teaspoon of the vanilla extract.

3. Line a baking sheet with 2 layers of heavy brown paper. Trace outline of loaf of bread, about 15 x 4 inches, on the paper. Using table knife, spread meringue within outline, building it up evenly. Bake for 1 hour and 15 minutes or until light beige on top. Cool completely on baking sheet on wire rack. The top will crack.

4. Meanwhile, use electric mixer at high speed to beat cream, 1 tablespoon superfine sugar and remaining 1 teaspoon vanilla extract in small bowl until stiff; chill. Make Buttercream Filling.

5. To assemble torte, cut meringue horizontally in half with serrated bread knife. Place bottom half on serving tray. Spread with half of Buttercream Filling. Tear angel food cake into tiny ½-inch tufts and push into buttercream; cover with remaining buttercream. Top with second meringue half.

6. Spread whipped cream frosting on top and sides to cover. Sprinkle with pecans mixed with any meringue crumbs. Refrigerate until serving time. Using serrated knife, slice diagonally. *Serves twelve to fourteen.*

Buttercream Filling

6 egg yolks
1 cup confectioners' sugar
1 tablespoon vanilla extract
one 6-ounce package semisweet chocolate morsels
2 tablespoons heavy cream
1 cup butter or margarine, softened

1. In top of double boiler, beat egg yolks, confectioners' sugar and vanilla extract until smooth. Place over hot (not boiling) water; using electric mixer at high speed, beat until thickened and increased in volume.

2. Melt chocolate in small saucepan over low heat; stir in cream. Add to yolk mixture and beat until well blended. Remove from heat and cool to room temperature. Using electric mixer at high speed, gradually beat in butter or margarine until well blended. *Makes about 2 cups.*

CHOCOLATE MERINGUE TORTE

MERINGUE
4 egg whites
⅛ teaspoon salt
1½ cups granulated sugar
¼ cup ground almonds

CHOCOLATE FILLING
2 egg whites
½ cup granulated sugar
1 cup butter or margarine,
    softened
four 1-ounce squares
    German sweet chocolate,
    melted
2 tablespoons cocoa powder
confectioners' sugar

1. Preheat oven to 250° F. Draw four 8-inch circles on freezer paper or parchment paper. Place paper on baking sheets.

2. To make meringue, use electric mixer at high speed to beat 4 egg whites and the salt in medium bowl until foamy-white and doubled in volume. Add 1½ cups granulated sugar, 1 tablespoon at a time, beating well after each addition; beat until stiff peaks form. Fold in ground almonds. Using table knife, spread meringue in circles outlined on paper.

3. Bake for 45 minutes. Turn off oven and leave meringues in oven with door open for 15 minutes. Carefully remove meringues from paper with sharp-edged spatula to wire rack and cool completely.

4. To make filling, use electric mixer at high speed to beat 2 egg whites in top of double boiler until foamy-white and doubled in volume. Place over hot (not boiling) water. Gradually beat in ½ cup granulated sugar, then butter or margarine, melted chocolate and cocoa. Remove from heat and cool to room temperature.

5. Place 1 meringue circle on serving plate; spread with one-third of filling. Repeat layers, ending with meringue circle. Sprinkle top with confectioners' sugar. Refrigerate until serving time. Use serrated knife to cut. *Serves eight.*

Good meringues are an impressive credit on your party-giving résumé. Be patient, and beat the egg whites as specified, adding sugar gradually and beating until whites are stiff but not dry; never underbeat. Don't open the oven door to sneak a look at your meringues before the baking time is up. And always cool them completely before assembling a torte like the one above and/or refrigerating meringues. Also avoid making them on a humid day; a combination of humidity and overbaking creates tough meringues.

SACHER TORTE

½ cup unsalted butter
7 ounces semisweet
  chocolate
8 egg yolks
1 teaspoon vanilla extract
10 egg whites
⅛ teaspoon salt
¾ cup sugar
1 cup sifted flour

GLAZE
three 1-ounce squares
  unsweetened chocolate,
  broken into pieces
1 cup heavy cream
1 cup sugar
1 teaspoon corn syrup
1 egg, beaten
1 teaspoon vanilla extract

¼ to ½ cup apricot jam

1. Preheat oven to 350° F. Grease and flour two 9-inch or three 8-inch cake pans.

2. Melt butter in medium saucepan over low heat; add semisweet chocolate and stir until melted. Remove pan from heat. Beat in egg yolks and 1 teaspoon vanilla extract until mixture is smooth and well blended. Cool.

3. Using electric mixer at high speed, beat egg whites and salt in large bowl until foamy. Gradually add ¾ cup sugar, beating until stiff, glossy peaks form.

4. Mix about 1 cup of the beaten egg whites into chocolate mixture until all white disappears. Slowly pour egg white mixture into chocolate mixture and fold together gently but completely.

5. Sprinkle flour, 4 to 5 tablespoons at a time, on top of chocolate mixture. Gently fold together until all flour is incorporated into batter. Spoon into prepared pans.

6. Bake for 30 to 40 minutes, until top springs back when lightly touched and edges of cake start to pull away from sides of pans. Cool in pans on wire rack for 10 minutes. Turn out onto rack and cool to room temperature.

7. Meanwhile, make glaze by mixing unsweetened chocolate, cream, 1 cup sugar and the corn syrup in medium saucepan. Place over low heat; stir until chocolate is melted. Raise heat to medium; cook and stir mixture for 5 minutes.

8. Add a few spoonfuls of chocolate mixture to beaten egg and mix well; return to mixture in pan. Mix well. Stir over low heat until mixture coats back of wooden spoon. Remove pan from heat; add 1 teaspoon vanilla extract and cool to room temperature.

9. When cake is cool, spread bottom layer(s) with apricot jam. Stack layers and spoon glaze over top and down sides. Refrigerate for about 3 hours to set glaze. Serve at room temperature. *Serves ten to twelve.*

Note: This is a very traditional recipe and one of the few in which only butter should be used.

STRAWBERRY TORTE

MERINGUE SHELL
10 egg whites
3⅓ cups granulated sugar
1½ teaspoons white vinegar

FILLING
1 envelope unflavored
    gelatin
2 tablespoons water
2 cups heavy cream
2 teaspoons superfine sugar
1 teaspoon vanilla extract
2 pints fresh strawberries,
    washed and hulled

1. Preheat oven to 275° F. Line 2 baking sheets with foil.

2. To make meringue shell, use electric mixer at high speed to beat 6 egg whites in large bowl until foamy-white and doubled in volume. Gradually beat in 2 cups of the granulated sugar, 1 tablespoon at a time, with 1 teaspoon of the vinegar, beating well after each addition. Beat until meringue is glossy and stiff peaks form.

3. Mark four 8-inch circles on foil-lined baking sheets, two on each sheet. Spread one-third of meringue in 1-inch-thick disk on one of the marked circles. Using 2 spoons, place remaining meringue in a ring on each of the other 3 circles. With a spatula, flatten top of each ring to allow rings to be stacked more easily.

4. Bake for 1 hour or until hard. Cool overnight.

5. Beat remaining 4 egg whites, remaining 1⅓ cups granulated sugar and ½ teaspoon vinegar as directed in Step 2 for first batch of meringue. Loosen the 8-inch disk and the 3 rings from foil. Place disk on a foil-lined baking sheet and stack 3 rings on top, cementing layers together with some of the meringue. Spread remaining meringue on sides and top of torte.

6. Bake for 1 hour. Cool for 2 to 3 hours, then fill.

7. To make filling, sprinkle gelatin over water in metal 1-cup measure. Place in skillet containing 1 inch simmering water; heat, stirring constantly, until gelatin is dissolved. Remove from heat and refrigerate until gelatin is consistency of unbeaten egg whites, about 20 minutes.

8. Using electric mixer at high speed, beat cream, syrupy gelatin, superfine sugar and vanilla extract in medium bowl until stiff. Reserve 10 to 12 strawberries for garnish, slicing half of them; slice remaining berries onto beaten cream mixture, and fold in gently.

9. Fill meringue shell with beaten cream mixture. Decorate top edge with reserved sliced strawberries. Garnish with strawberries cut into fan shapes. Refrigerate until serving time. *Serves ten. Pictured on page 52.*

FUDGE RIBBON BARS

2 tablespoons butter or margarine
2¼ cups sugar
1 tablespoon cornstarch
one 8-ounce package cream cheese
3 eggs
2 tablespoons milk
1 teaspoon vanilla extract
2 cups sifted flour
1 teaspoon salt
1 teaspoon baking powder
½ teaspoon baking soda
½ cup butter or margarine, softened
1½ cups milk
four 1-ounce squares unsweetened chocolate, melted
1 teaspoon vanilla extract
Fudge Frosting (below)

1. Preheat oven to 350° F. Grease and flour 13 x 9 x 2-inch baking pan.

2. In medium bowl, cream 2 tablespoons butter or margarine with ¼ cup of the sugar and the cornstarch. Beat in cream cheese, 1 egg, 2 tablespoons milk and 1 teaspoon vanilla extract. Mix until smooth and creamy; set aside.

3. In large bowl, mix flour, remaining 2 cups sugar, the salt, baking powder and baking soda. Using electric mixer at medium speed, beat in ½ cup butter or margarine and 1½ cups milk. Continue to beat until very smooth and creamy. Beat in remaining 2 eggs, the melted chocolate and 1 teaspoon vanilla extract.

4. Pour about two-thirds of batter into prepared pan; spread with reserved cheese mixture. Spread remaining chocolate batter on top. Bake for about 50 minutes, until cake tester inserted in center comes out clean. Cool in pan on wire rack for 10 minutes, then turn out onto rack and cool completely.

5. Meanwhile, prepare Fudge Frosting; use to frost top of cooled cake. Cut cake into 2 x 1½-inch bars. *Makes 36.*

Fudge Frosting

⅓ cup milk
¼ cup butter or margarine
one 6-ounce package semisweet chocolate morsels
2¼ cups confectioners' sugar
1 teaspoon vanilla extract

1. In small saucepan, combine milk and butter or margarine; bring to boiling point over medium heat. Reduce heat to low; add chocolate and stir until melted and smooth.

2. Beat in confectioners' sugar and vanilla extract. Remove from heat; continue to beat until mixture reaches spreading consistency. If necessary, add a few drops of milk. *Makes enough for one 13 x 9 x 2-inch cake.*

CHOCOLATE POTS DE CREME

2 cups light cream or
   half-and-half
1 cup heavy cream
one 12-ounce package
   semisweet chocolate
   morsels
9 egg yolks
⅓ cup brandy

TOPPING
1 cup heavy cream
1 tablespoon sugar
1 teaspoon vanilla extract

1. In medium saucepan, scald light cream or half-and-half and 1 cup heavy cream over low heat. Remove from heat and add chocolate; stir until melted.

2. In electric blender, process egg yolks and brandy at high speed for 30 seconds or until well blended.

3. Strain chocolate mixture through fine sieve into large pouring cup or pitcher. With blender motor on, gradually pour mixture into blender through feed opening in cap, blending until well combined with egg yolk mixture.

4. Pour into 12 pots de crème containers or small wine glasses, or 1 large glass serving bowl. Cover with lids or plastic wrap; refrigerate at least 6 hours or overnight.

5. At serving time, make topping by using electric mixer at high speed to beat 1 cup heavy cream, the sugar and vanilla extract in small bowl until stiff. Pass in bowl or spoon a large swirl onto each serving. *Serves twelve.*

GRAND GALA DESSERT

3 cups crushed macaroons
1 cup bourbon or rum
2 cups butter or margarine
2 cups sugar
12 eggs yolks
four 1-ounce squares
   unsweetened chocolate,
   melted and cooled
1 teaspoon vanilla extract
1 cup chopped pecans
24 ladyfingers, split
1 cup heavy cream
semisweet chocolate curls,
   from one 1-ounce square

1. Soak macaroons in bourbon or rum.

2. In large bowl, cream butter or margarine and sugar until light and fluffy. Add egg yolks one at a time, beating well after each addition. Add melted chocolate, vanilla extract and chopped pecans; stir to blend well.

3. Line bottom and side of 10-inch springform pan with split ladyfingers. Fill with alternate layers of soaked macaroons and chocolate mixture. Chill at least 8 hours or overnight.

4. At serving time, remove side of pan. Beat cream until stiff; swirl on top of cake. Decorate with chocolate curls. *Serves twelve to sixteen.*

MERINGUE SHELLS WITH RASPBERRY-GINGER CREAM

MERINGUE SHELLS
7 egg whites
2 cups granulated sugar
½ teaspoon salt
1 teaspoon vanilla extract

RASPBERRY-GINGER CREAM
2 cups heavy cream
1 quart fresh or frozen
raspberries
1 tablespoon brown sugar
1 teaspoon ginger

1. Preheat oven to 225° F. Line baking sheet with brown paper. Mark twelve 4-inch rounds on paper.

2. To make meringue shells, use electric mixer at high speed to beat egg whites in large bowl until foamy-white and doubled in volume. Mix granulated sugar with salt and add, 1 tablespoon at a time, beating constantly until sugar dissolves and mixture forms stiff peaks. Fold in vanilla extract.

3. Drop onto rounds on lined baking sheet. With spoon, swirl meringues to form decorative shells.

4. Bake for 45 to 60 minutes, or until meringues are firm but still white. Cool for 5 minutes on baking sheet on wire rack. Carefully remove with wide spatula onto wire rack; cool completely.

5. Just before serving, make raspberry-ginger cream by beating cream in deep chilled bowl until stiff. Fold in berries, brown sugar and ginger. Fill meringue shells with mixture. *Serves twelve.*

Note: Meringues can be baked several days ahead and stored in cookie tins.

APRICOT SOUFFLE WITH CUSTARD SAUCE

¼ cup sugar
one 16-ounce can unpeeled
apricot halves, drained
¼ cup lemon juice
8 egg whites
¼ teaspoon cream of tartar
Custard Sauce (page 140)

1. Preheat oven to 350° F. Butter 12-inch straight-sided soufflé dish; sprinkle with 1 tablespoon of the sugar. Fit with 3-inch waxed paper collar; butter collar.

2. In electric blender, process drained apricots, lemon juice and remaining 3 tablespoons sugar on high speed for 30 seconds or until pureed.

3. Using electric mixer at high speed, beat egg whites with cream of tartar in medium bowl until stiff peaks form. Carefully fold into apricot puree. Spoon into prepared dish. Place in roasting pan on oven rack; fill pan with 1 inch hot water.

4. Bake for 35 minutes or until soufflé is well risen, puffed and slightly brown on top. Serve immediately with Custard Sauce. *Serves eight.*

Custard Sauce

6 egg yolks
¼ cup sugar
⅛ teaspoon salt
2¼ cups milk
1 teaspoon vanilla extract

1. Lightly beat egg yolks with wire whisk in top of double boiler. Beat in sugar and salt until mixture is thick and lemon colored.

2. Scald milk in small saucepan; stir a little into beaten yolk mixture. Place over hot (not boiling) water. Slowly add remaining milk, beating constantly with wire whisk. Cook, beating constantly, until mixture thickens.

3. Strain mixture into small bowl; cool. Stir in vanilla extract. Refrigerate until serving time. *Makes approximately 3 cups.*

LIME-MOCHA MOUSSE STRATA

LIME MOUSSE
1 envelope unflavored gelatin
¼ cup cold water
3 egg yolks
1½ cups superfine sugar
1 teaspoon grated lime rind
½ cup fresh lime juice
1 drop green food coloring (optional)

MOCHA MOUSSE
½ cup butter or margarine
2 tablespoons instant espresso coffee powder, dissolved in ½ cup boiling water
2 cups cocoa powder
4 egg yolks
1½ cups superfine sugar
½ cup orange liqueur

7 egg whites
⅛ teaspoon salt
3 cups heavy cream
additional beaten cream, candied violets, chopped pistachios (optional)

1. To make lime mousse, sprinkle gelatin over cold water in small bowl to soften. Using electric mixer at high speed, beat 3 egg yolks in medium bowl until light in color. Gradually add 1½ cups sugar and beat until ribbon forms when beaters are lifted. Stir in lime rind.

2. Heat lime juice in small saucepan until very hot but not bubbling. Add to softened gelatin and stir until gelatin dissolves. Stir into egg yolk mixture; add green food coloring if desired. Refrigerate until mixture is consistency of unbeaten egg whites, about 20 minutes, stirring every 5 minutes.

3. Meanwhile, make mocha mousse by melting butter or margarine in top of double boiler over hot (not boiling) water. Add coffee, then cocoa, beating constantly with wire whisk until smooth paste forms.

4. Using electric mixer at high speed, beat 4 egg yolks in large bowl until light in color. Gradually add 1½ cups sugar, beating until ribbon forms when beaters are lifted. Slowly beat cocoa mixture into egg yolk mixture, ½ cup at a time. Stir in liqueur. Wash beaters very well.

5. Using electric mixer at high speed, beat egg whites and salt in large bowl until stiff. Beat 3 cups cream in another bowl until stiff. Fold one-third of beaten cream into lime mousse, two-thirds into mocha mousse.

6. Carefully fold one-half of beaten egg whites into mocha mousse; pour half of mixture into glass serving bowl. Fold remaining whites into lime mousse; pour over mocha mousse in bowl. Add remaining mocha mousse. Cover with plastic wrap and refrigerate for at least 3 hours. Decorate with rosettes of beaten cream, candied violets and pistachios if desired. *Serves twelve to fourteen.*

BLACK FOREST SOUFFLE

one 16-ounce can sour pie
  cherries, drained
6 tablespoons kirsch
four 1-ounce squares
  semisweet chocolate
2 envelopes unflavored
  gelatin
1 cup sugar
3 eggs, separated
2 cups milk
1½ teaspoons vanilla extract
2 cups heavy cream

1. Reserve ½ cup of the drained cherries for garnish. Chop remaining cherries and marinate in 3 tablespoons of the kirsch. Hold 1 square of the chocolate in palm of hand to soften slightly. Make chocolate curls for garnish by shaving vegetable peeler across chocolate, using about one-fourth of square. Place curls on baking sheet and refrigerate until serving time.

2. In medium saucepan, mix gelatin and ½ cup of the sugar. Add egg yolks, milk and remaining chocolate. Cook over low heat, stirring constantly, until chocolate melts and gelatin dissolves; remove from heat. Add remaining 3 tablespoons kirsch and the vanilla extract; beat until smooth and well blended. Refrigerate until mixture is consistency of unbeaten egg whites, about 45 minutes.

3. Using electric mixer at high speed, beat egg whites in small bowl until soft peaks form. Add remaining ½ cup sugar, 1 tablespoon at a time, beating well after each addition; beat until stiff peaks form. Fold meringue into syrupy chocolate mixture.

4. Using electric mixer at high speed, beat 1½ cups of the cream in another small bowl until stiff. Fold into chocolate mixture, then fold in chopped cherries. Pour into 2-quart soufflé dish or 1½-quart soufflé dish with aluminum foil collar. Refrigerate for at least 4 hours or overnight.

5. At serving time, beat remaining ½ cup cream, place in pastry bag and pipe around top of soufflé; garnish with chocolate curls and whole cherries. *Serves ten.*

DAIQUIRI SOUFFLE

10 eggs, separated
2 cups sugar
⅓ cup lime juice
⅓ cup lemon juice
⅓ cup orange juice
2 teaspoons finely grated lime rind
2 teaspoons finely grated lemon rind
⅛ teaspoon salt
2 envelopes unflavored gelatin
½ cup light rum
3 cups heavy cream
sliced almonds
lime twist

1. Beat egg yolks and 1 cup of the sugar in top of large double boiler over simmering water. Add lime, lemon and orange juice, lime and lemon rind and salt. Using wire whisk, stir until mixture thickens.

2. Soften gelatin in rum; stir into egg yolk mixture until gelatin is dissolved. Remove from heat and let cool.

3. Using electric mixer at high speed, beat egg whites in large bowl until foamy. Gradually add remaining 1 cup sugar; beat until stiff.

4. Beat 2 cups of the cream in large bowl until stiff. Fold egg white meringue into cooled custard, then fold in beaten cream.

5. Wrap a 3-inch foil or waxed paper collar around top of 1½-quart soufflé dish; lightly oil collar. Spoon soufflé mixture into dish and chill for several hours or overnight, until firm.

6. When ready to serve, carefully remove collar. Beat remaining 1 cup cream until stiff; use to decorate top of soufflé. Sprinkle top and sides with sliced almonds. Garnish with twist of lime. *Serves twelve.*

AMBROSIA

½ cup heavy cream, stiffly beaten
½ cup sour cream
one 3½-ounce can coconut
1 cup miniature marshmallows
3 cups orange sections

1. In medium bowl, gently combine stiffly beaten cream, sour cream, coconut and marshmallows.

2. Place orange sections in medium-size crystal bowl. Fold in two-thirds of cream mixture until well blended. Top with remaining cream mixture. Refrigerate until serving time. *Serves four to six.*

FRIED APPLES

6 large Winesap apples, cored
2 tablespoons butter or margarine
⅔ cup sugar
⅛ teaspoon salt
⅔ cup water

1. Cut apples crosswise into ⅓-inch-thick slices. Melt butter or margarine in large skillet over medium heat; add apples. Sprinkle with sugar and salt; add water.

2. Cover skillet and cook 10 minutes, stirring frequently. Remove lid and simmer, stirring, until water evaporates and apples are caramelized; do not burn. *Serves six.*

BANANAS FLAMBE

½ cup butter or margarine
½ cup brown sugar, firmly
  packed
4 firm-ripe bananas
½ teaspoon cinnamon
1 cup white rum
1½ pints vanilla ice cream

1. Heat butter or margarine and brown sugar in chafing dish until sugar is melted. Peel bananas and cut lengthwise in half.

2. Add halved bananas to syrup. Cook until banana halves are golden, carefully turning and spooning syrup over fruit. Sprinkle with cinnamon; add rum, taking care not to stir into syrup. Heat through, at least 2 to 3 minutes.

3. Flame rum, then stir and spoon sauce over bananas until flame goes out. Serve with large scoops of vanilla ice cream. *Serves four.*

PEACHES CARDINAL

7 cups water
2 cups sugar
2 tablespoons vanilla extract
10 large firm peaches
two 10-ounce packages
  frozen raspberries,
  thawed

1. In large saucepan, combine water, 1½ cups of the sugar and the vanilla extract; bring to boiling point over medium heat. Reduce heat to low and simmer until sugar is dissolved.

2. Add peaches to simmering syrup; simmer for 8 minutes. Remove from heat and cool peaches in syrup for 20 minutes. Drain and peel peaches.

3. Arrange peaches in large glass or silver serving dish. (Or halve and pit peaches; place 2 halves in each of 10 champagne glasses.) Cover with plastic wrap and refrigerate for at least 1 hour or until serving time.

4. Press thawed berries through fine sieve into container of electric blender; add remaining ½ cup sugar. Process at high speed for 1 minute or until mixture is thick and sugar is dissolved. Refrigerate; at serving time, spoon puree over peaches. *Serves ten.*

Note: Two 32-ounce cans peach halves in heavy syrup, drained, may be substituted for the fresh peaches. Follow recipe from Step 3 on.

PEARS WITH SABAYON SAUCE

4 cups cold water
1 tablespoon lemon juice
4 large firm pears
4 cups water
½ cup sugar
1 orange
Sabayon Sauce (below)

1. In large bowl, mix 4 cups cold water and the lemon juice. Peel, halve and core pears; place in water-lemon juice mixture.

2. Bring 4 cups water and the sugar to boiling point in large saucepan. Drain pears and add to syrup. Reduce heat to low and simmer for 10 minutes or until tender but not mushy. Cool pears in syrup; drain from syrup and refrigerate until serving time.

3. Peel orange, avoiding white pith; reserve orange for another use. Cut peel into very thin strips. Blanch in boiling water for 4 minutes; drain.

4. Make Sabayon Sauce. At serving time, place 1 pear half in each of 8 stemmed glass sherbet bowls. Spoon Sabayon Sauce over pears; garnish with orange strips. *Serves eight.*

Sabayon Sauce

⅓ cup sugar
3 egg yolks
1 egg white
¼ cup dry white wine
2 tablespoons orange
   liqueur

1. In top of double boiler, beat sugar, egg yolks and egg white with wire whisk until smooth. Place over hot (not boiling) water. Continue beating for a few seconds.

2. Slowly add wine and continue beating until sauce is tripled in volume. Remove from heat; add liqueur. Refrigerate until serving time. *Makes about 1⅓ cups*

ALEXANDER DESSERT

½ cup vanilla ice cream
2 tablespoons white crème
   de cacao
1 tablespoon brandy
cocoa powder

1. In electric blender, process ice cream, crème de cacao and brandy at high speed for 30 seconds or until smooth and thick.

2. Pour into 2 stemmed cocktail glasses. Sprinkle tops with cocoa powder and serve immediately. *Serves two.*

ORANGE ELEGANCE DESSERT

¼ cup vanilla ice cream
¼ cup orange sherbet
2 tablespoons light rum
1 tablespoon white crème de
   cacao
1 tablespoon orange liqueur
2 orange slices

1. In electric blender, process ice cream, sherbet, rum, crème de cacao and orange liqueur at high speed for 30 seconds or until smooth and thick.

2. Pour into 2 stemmed cocktail glasses. Garnish each with orange slice and serve immediately. *Serves two.*

FROZEN DAISY DESSERT

18 ladyfingers, split
¼ cup ground almonds
2 quarts mocha ice cream,
    softened
one 10-ounce jar chocolate
    sauce

1. Line bottom of 3-quart charlotte mold or any other flat-bottomed mold with waxed paper. Arrange split ladyfingers on bottom of pan to form 6-petal daisy. Stand remaining ladyfingers around edge.

2. Sprinkle 1 tablespoon of the almonds on daisy. Add one-third of softened ice cream, packing into a firm layer. Drizzle on ½ cup of the chocolate sauce. Sprinkle with 1 tablespoon almonds. Repeat with one-third of ice cream, ½ cup of the sauce and 1 tablespoon almonds; top with last third of ice cream and reserve remaining sauce and nuts. Cover mold; freeze at least 6 hours or overnight.

3. Remove from freezer at least 30 minutes before serving. Run a thin-bladed knife around edge of mold; invert onto footed serving platter. Place in refrigerator. Just before serving, drizzle reserved chocolate sauce across daisy; sprinkle reserved almonds on top. *Serves twelve.*

CAFE BRULOT

peel of ½ orange, cut into
    strips
peel of ½ lemon, cut into
    strips
8 whole cloves
5 sugar cubes
2 whole allspice berries
two 2-inch cinnamon sticks
1½ cups brandy
3 cups very strong hot coffee

1. In chafing dish, combine orange peel, lemon peel, cloves, sugar cubes, allspice, cinnamon sticks and brandy. Heat and stir for 1 to 2 minutes to blend flavors, melt sugar and warm brandy.

2. Using match or taper, flame brandy. As mixture flames, gradually add coffee. Serve very hot after flame subsides. *Makes 6 demitasse servings.*

CAFE DE MINTA

2 teaspoons instant coffee
    powder
½ teaspoon peppermint
    extract
about 1½ cups boiling water
½ cup heavy cream, stiffly
    beaten and sweetened
1 teaspoon green crème de
    menthe

1. Divide coffee powder and peppermint extract among 4 demitasse cups. Add boiling water to fill cups about three-fourths full; stir.

2. Top each with beaten cream; drizzle a little crème de menthe on top of cream. *Makes 4 demitasse servings.*

CAFE VIENNESE

3 coffee measures coffee grounds
3 cups water
1 teaspoon cinnamon
½ teaspoon nutmeg
¼ teaspoon allspice
⅛ teaspoon cloves
½ cup heavy cream, stiffly beaten and sweetened
chocolate curls

1. Using favorite method, brew together coffee, water, cinnamon, nutmeg, allspice and cloves. When strong as desired, strain into warmed pot.

2. Serve hot, topped with beaten heavy cream and sprinkled with chocolate curls. *Makes 6 demitasse servings.*

CAPPUCCINO

2 cups hot milk
2 cups very strong hot espresso coffee
cinnamon

1. Heat milk in small saucepan until bubbles form around edge. Pour into blender container and process for 1 minute or until very frothy.

2. Mix coffee and milk; pour into warmed cups. Sprinkle with cinnamon. *Serves four.*

INSTANT SPICED TEA FOR A CROWD

one 18-ounce jar orange instant breakfast drink
1½ cups sugar
1 cup instant tea with lemon
1½ teaspoons cloves
1½ teaspoons cinnamon
boiling water

1. In large bowl, combine instant breakfast drink, sugar, instant tea, cloves and cinnamon until well blended. Store in airtight container.

2. For each serving, place 2 teaspoons spiced tea mix in cup; fill cup with boiling water. *Serves 100.*

PREVIEW PUNCH

1 quart strong tea
1 quart soda water
1 quart dark rum
2 cups sugar
peel of 12 lemons, cut into thin strips
juice of 12 lemons (¾ cup)
2 tablespoons brandy
ice cubes

In large punch bowl, blend tea, soda water, rum, sugar, lemon peel, lemon juice and brandy. Add ice cubes and serve immediately. *Serves twenty.*

HOT BUTTERED RUM

FOR TWO
1 cup apple cider
1 teaspoon brown sugar
2 sticks cinnamon
4 whole cloves
½ cup light rum
¼ cup dark Jamaican rum
2 tablespoons butter

FOR A CROWD (16 to 20)
1 gallon apple cider
1 cup brown sugar, firmly
   packed
½ box stick cinnamon
1 tablespoon whole cloves
2 fifths light rum
1 fifth dark Jamaican rum
½ cup butter

1. In saucepan, combine cider, brown sugar, cinnamon and cloves. Bring to boiling point; reduce heat to low. Add light rum and dark rum. Heat but do not boil.

2. Pour into heated mugs. Add stick of cinnamon to each; top each with a pat of butter.

SANGRIA

1 orange, sliced
1 lemon, sliced
1 tray ice cubes
one 24-ounce bottle
   Burgundy wine
one 10-ounce bottle soda
   water
1 cup orange juice
½ cup lemon juice
½ cup cognac (optional)
½ cup rum (optional)
½ cup sugar
additional lemon or orange
   slices

1. Place slices from 1 orange and 1 lemon in large glass pitcher. Add ice.

2. Pour in wine, soda water, orange juice and lemon juice; add cognac and rum if desired, and pour in sugar. Stir vigorously until well blended.

3. Serve in tall glasses, garnished with an additional slice of lemon or orange. *Serves four to six.*

HOT SPICED WINE

1 quart Burgundy wine
1 cup sugar
4 oranges, sliced
4 lemons, sliced
8 whole cloves
four 3-inch cinnamon sticks,
   broken

1. In large saucepan, combine wine, sugar, orange slices, lemon slices, cloves and cinnamon stick pieces.

2. Heat over low heat for 10 minutes or until sugar is dissolved and mixture is hot, stirring once or twice. Serve in mugs. *Serves four to six.*

FOXY LADY HIGHBALL

2 ounces (¼ cup) dark rum
1 ounce (2 tablespoons)
  anise liqueur
ice cubes
soda water or sparkling
  mineral water
¼ lemon

Pour rum and anise liqueur over ice in a tall 10- or 12-ounce glass. Fill with soda water or mineral water. Squeeze lemon into glass. *Serves one.*

FRENCH #75

1½ teaspoons lemon juice
1 to 2 teaspoons superfine
  sugar
2 ounces (¼ cup) cognac
ice cubes
split of champagne

Place lemon juice in tall 10- or 12-ounce glass. Add sugar and stir until dissolved. Add cognac and ice. Slowly pour in champagne to fill glass. *Serves one.*

SHANDY GAFF

one 12-ounce bottle beer,
  chilled
one 10-ounce bottle ginger
  beer, chilled
1 lime, quartered

Combine beer and ginger beer in pitcher. Add quartered lime and stir well. *Serves two.*

INDEX